Journalism Between t and the Market

Using the Nordic media model as an empirical backdrop, *Journalism Between the State and the Market* defines and analyzes journalism's fundamental problem: its shifting location between the state and the market.

This book examines how this distance is decreasing as journalism steps closer to both the market (algorithmically monetizing audiences) and the state (lobbying governments for subsidies and attacking public service broadcasting). The book analyzes journalism's negotiated position between the market and the state in the age of disruptions, offering a theoretical foundation that seeks to account for the structural conditions of journalism in the digital age.

For scholars, graduates and students in journalism, news sociology and media and communication studies, *Journalism Between the State and the Market* provides a theoretical perspective that can be used as a valuable tool when studying and observing the current developments in journalism.

Helle Sjøvaag is Professor of Journalism at the University of Stavanger, Norway. Her research areas include digital journalism, media diversity and media systems and regulation. Sjøvaag has published extensively in international journals, including *Journalism & Mass Communication Quarterly*; *Media, Culture & Society*; *Journalism Studies*; *Convergence* and *Journal of Media Business Studies*. Sjøvaag's most recent book is the co-edited anthology *Journalism Re-examined: Digital Challenges and Professional Reorientations: Lessons From Northern Europe*.

Disruptions: Studies in Digital Journalism
Series editor: Bob Franklin

Disruptions refers to the radical changes provoked by the affordances of digital technologies that occur at a pace and on a scale that disrupts settled understandings and traditional ways of creating value, interacting and communicating both socially and professionally. The consequences for digital journalism involve far-reaching changes to business models, professional practices, roles, ethics, products and even challenges to the accepted definitions and understandings of journalism. For Digital Journalism Studies, the field of academic inquiry which explores and examines digital journalism, disruption results in paradigmatic and tectonic shifts in scholarly concerns. It prompts reconsideration of research methods, theoretical analyses and responses (oppositional and consensual) to such changes, which have been described as being akin to 'a moment of mind-blowing uncertainty'.

Routledge's new book series, ***Disruptions: Studies in Digital Journalism***, seeks to capture, examine and analyse these moments of exciting and explosive professional and scholarly innovation which characterize developments in the day-to-day practice of journalism in an age of digital media, and which are articulated in the newly emerging academic discipline of Digital Journalism Studies.

Data Journalism and the Regeneration of News
Alfred Hermida and Mary Lynn Young

A Short History of Disruptive Journalism Technologies
1960–1990
Will Mari

Journalism Between the State and the Market
Helle Sjøvaag

For more information, please visit: www.routledge.com/Disruptions/book-series/DISRUPTDIGJOUR

Journalism Between the State and the Market

Helle Sjøvaag

LONDON AND NEW YORK

First published 2019 by Routledge

2 Park Square, Milton Park, Abingdon, Oxon OX14 4RN
605 Third Avenue, New York, NY 10017

Routledge is an imprint of the Taylor & Francis Group, an informa business

First issued in paperback 2022

Publisher's Note

The publisher has gone to great lengths to ensure the quality of this reprint but points out that some imperfections in the original copies may be apparent.

British Library Cataloguing-in-Publication Data
A catalogue record for this book is available from the British Library

Library of Congress Cataloging-in-Publication Data
A catalog record for this book has been requested

ISBN: 978-1-138-54334-8 (hbk)
ISBN: 978-1-03-233843-9 (pbk)
DOI: 10.4324/9781351035347

Typeset in Times New Roman
by Apex CoVantage, LLC

Contents

Preface

The idea for this book emerged during the International Communication Association's Journalism Studies Division reception in San Diego in May 2017. This is one of those academic venues where journalism studies shows its versatility: normative as well as analytical, close to industry concerns yet distanced from industry realities. This is because many journalism scholars have a background in journalism. They have felt the profession – its problems as well as its promises – in their bones. Professional association with the object of study, some kind of felt experience, is still something that gives legitimacy to journalism scholars – not just in the industry but also within the research community. I have always felt slightly uncomfortable about this closeness between the observers and what is observed. It's not like any of the other professional sociologies have this proclivity; political scientists do not need to have political experience to be seen as legitimate scholars of political science. Perhaps my discomfort stems from the fact that I don't have this experience, and as a result, I feel my observations are somehow less legitimate, as they are not checked by experienced reality.

I have, nevertheless, been engaged in journalism research since the early 2000s. Throughout my career, the main focus in journalism studies at large has been its "crisis" – mainly the disruption caused by digitalization, but also its decline from economic gold mine (owning a newspaper used to be a license to print money, so to speak) to all-but-harvest-worthy dead horse (the newspaper being analogous to horse carts as cars emerged in the early 20th century). Fifteen years of observation isn't a long time, by any means, but throughout these observations, relating my research at academic conferences has always left me with an unsettling feeling that something has been overlooked. Whenever we talk about the source of this crisis, money always emerges as the great culprit: economic motives as a great evil. It seems odd to me that what is essentially a reality – the economy – should be condemned so normatively. In the endeavor to seek social explanations for the state of things, shouldn't money be viewed with the same methodological neutrality as other factors, instead of as some predetermined evil? Money, for journalism, is a necessity. And it is a good necessity: it frees journalism from the state – basically the narrative history behind journalism's entire legitimacy.

This book seeks to bring money into the sociological view of journalism with less of a suspicious attachment to its corrupting potential. The idea is a simple one: journalism's problem is its position between the state and the market. It needs to retain its distance from both, or its boundaries will be threatened. When journalism approaches one of them, its legitimacy is weakened. Corrections can, however, be made when distances grow to short, restoring the balance. Journalism's problem now is that it is approaching both fields at the same time. Content marketing and personalization brings journalism closer to the market. Increased state support and protectionism brings it closer to the state. The problem resides in this dual proximity, making it hard to adjust in either direction, with everything being so close.

Journalism's position between the market and the state is a rather fundamental idea in journalism studies. As part of the public sphere, this ideal is firmly embedded in both political economy and political science. The problem with theory – an explanatory model that can be used to analyze the state of things – is its invitation to universality. Universality is very difficult to attain with journalism, especially in a state/market context that is so dependent on national or regional particularities. Moreover, empirically, this can never be more than a snapshot of trends and tendencies. It's not easy to do research on a fast-moving target. So, in order to do this, it has to be in a context with which I'm familiar, with a methodological approach I can handle, based on a theoretical framework I know.

The solution to how to package this idea came when Bob Franklin, the series editor, asked if I was interested in proposing a book for his *Disruption* series. The series has a short-format, snapshot-oriented focus on current developments in journalism around the globe with a quick production turnaround driven by a mission to get new research published fast. Moreover, the format is attractive because it speaks to an audience of researchers already engaged in the field. This allows me to take a lot for granted, which makes the writing process far more enjoyable – not to say manageable for someone predominantly used to the article format. Hence, this book is an attempt at a model that explains something about journalism, based on a simple idea, backed by examples from the Scandinavian context, within a media systems framework. As such, the book draws on work conducted within a research project I am currently leading at the University of Stavanger: digital news agendas in Scandinavia. The project is funded by the Swedish Ander Foundation and aims to investigate the impact of digital infrastructures on journalism as an institution in a Nordic media model context. This project involves two important collaborators in particular: Professor Michael Karlsson at Karlstad University in Sweden, and Associate Professor Aske Kammer at the IT University of Copenhagen in Denmark. Many of the insights shared in this volume derive from work with these two excellent colleagues.

Once the format was set and reviewers convinced, so began the arduous but enjoyable work of reading prior research and collecting some sort of data. For the first time in years, I read entire books cover to cover. One particularly important contribution in conducting the research for this book was David Ryfe's *Journalism and the Public* (Wiley & Sons, 2017). In a sense, Ryfe's work is so thoughtful, convincing and comprehensive that it largely renders my own modest contribution redundant. Ryfe not only builds a convincing framework explaining the pressures on journalism but also focuses on one important component that is often missing in this kind of work: the public. Not only that, he explains professionalism as a force, pushing back against the pressures of the state and the market. Reading Ryfe's work made me initially consider whether to even bother continuing, but his study is focused on the American situation. So, I assured myself that perhaps a European, or more specifically, a Scandinavian perspective might make some addition to the field. The Scandinavian media systems are, after all, often highlighted by American scholars as particularly robust, especially in a state/market perspective. Not least, Scandinavian journalism is more or less equally pushed and pulled by these two fields, being mixed media systems. Lastly, I would also recommend this book to readers because it assumes a different theoretical vantage point; Ryfe's book assumes a field perspective, and I assume a media systems perspective – one that I think deserves reiteration after years of being criticized for being too generalist and too nation-bound.

I therefore thank David Ryfe for writing such an inspiring and important book (Ryfe was, incidentally, a member of my dissertation committee). I therefore hope to have added at least a Scandinavian footnote to his considerable contribution – one to which I also owe thanks to my project collaborators Michael Karlsson and Aske Kammer. I thank the Ander Foundation for the funding that has allowed me the time and opportunity to conduct this research, and I thank subsequent collaborators for their support: Truls André Pedersen, Eirik Stavelin, Wouter van Atteveldt, Mario Haim, Thomas Owren, Raul Ferrer Conill, Julie Mejse Münter Lassen and Malgorzata Anna Pachoczyk. Thanks also to the University of Stavanger for facilitating the process and for creating the environment for conducting the project. Not least, thanks to Bob Franklin for helping to shape this into a publishable form.

Lastly, a short note about data and methodology. The main method used in this research is literature review and document analysis. This basically means that I've been reading things, then sorting and synthesizing literature, policy documents and industry reports into context. The main empirical sources include the comprehensive media policy database hosted by Nordicom, the Norwegian media database hosted by Medienorge and the Scandinavian media trade press: *Journalisten* and *Kampanje* in Norway, *Journalisten*, *Mandag Morgen* and *Mediawatch* in Denmark, and *Dagens Media* and *Dagens Industri* in Sweden. Context and background on the Scandinavian media system are based on research conducted predominantly by Scandinavian scholars as well as media systems researchers. Besides these sources, many of the generalizations in this book are based on my prior research on journalism in the Nordic context, evidence of which you can find in my prior publications.

Stavanger, January 2019

1 Journalism's problem

Journalism's fundamental and enduring problem is its position between the state and the market. Journalism, as an institution, as a business and as a public good, sits between the legal entity that is the state and the economic entity that is the market. Journalism's social contract gives to the press the responsibility of overseeing the ruling powers on behalf of the citizenry. This gives considerable power to the journalistic institution. To ensure its legitimacy in this endeavor, journalism needs to maintain an appropriate distance from the state. The established arrangement for obtaining this distance is private ownership, secured through freedom of publication and freedom of expression. Journalism resides here – between the institution that legitimizes its power and the institution that renders it operational as such a power. These two institutions, however, serve as oppositional pulls on journalism. The danger in this position is sometimes referred to as the market failure thesis – the assertion that journalism cannot fully utilize the benefits of the market without hurting its public service. Journalism, however, cannot exist without either.

Journalism's fundamental problem is therefore how to maintain the proper distance between itself and these two fields. Get too close to the state, and fourth estate legitimacy is compromised. Get too close to the market, and professional legitimacy is compromised. Journalism's traditional business model has been based on this balance. Moreover, criticisms of journalism can often be traced to this problematic position. Attraction to the market conditions some forms of journalism that ensure commercial viability (sports, entertainment, consumer journalism etc.), which ensure the resources necessary to cover the state. At the same time, the draw of the market is precarious. Purely commercial news values are not wholly commensurate with democratically relevant journalism. At the same time, ties to the state can make certain forms of journalism possible, such as public service broadcasting. This also involves risk, however, as state subsidies, party ownership and state ownership are associated with political strings.

Journalism's current problem is that its distance to both fields is decreasing simultaneously. Although journalism's distance to these sectors has seen various degrees of closeness depending on historical and socio-political contexts, it is this dual proximity that suggests disruption. This balance is upset by digitalization, in particular: social media and third-party intermediaries. With the disruption of its dual income model (copy sales and advertising revenues), journalism has stepped closer to the market, specifically with algorithms collecting data on its users to personalize advertising, news diets and content marketing. At the same time, it moves closer to the legal institutions it is tasked with monitoring: differentiating towards more stable political segments to secure a subscription base, lobbying governments for incumbent-protecting subsidies or attacking public service broadcasting, organizations known for benchmarking quality standards in media markets. In trying to make up for losses in its advertising- and subscription-based funding model, journalism is drawn towards both spheres. As a result, the "neutral", institutional middle is weakening.

Let's begin to unpack some of the elements identified in journalism's problem. The two conflicting positions that journalism must balance are its institutional and economic identities. On the one hand, journalism serves as a fourth estate, overseeing the state and power sectors through a social contract that sustains the legitimacy of its publication powers. The type of critical journalism that supports democracy is undertaken for the benefit of the citizenry, legitimized through a system of professionalism that binds journalists to certain ethics, standards and procedures. This is journalism's institutional foundation, administered through the border patrolling mechanisms embedded in the boundary-maintaining properties of the profession. On the other hand, journalism is a business sustained by private ownership. As all owners have interests, and these interests inevitably affect the framework conditions under which journalism is performed, how these interests are served affects journalism's ability to maintain its professional boundaries. Embedded in private media ownership are two essential aims: earnings and influence. Although the influence sought may be ideal as well as ideological – either aiming to strengthen democracy or aiming to strengthen a certain political idea – earnings is a rather straightforward goal.

Because unprofitable business is unsustainable, journalistic enterprises need to make money. How that money is made indicates what degree of disruption we are talking about. While quality journalism can indeed be expected to attract enough paying customers to sustain a costly investigative news operation, more often than not, audiences are attracted to the distractions offered by the press – entertainment, lifestyle, celebrity, drama. This is when market failure can occur, when the investments needed to fulfill the social contract fail to justify the cost. But journalism also needs another source of income. Journalism's main sources of funding have always been the interests that seek news reading, and ultimately purchasing or voting, audiences: advertisers selling consumer goods or ideologues selling either a political message or an ideology. One financial attraction is the market, where growth is the main goal; the other is the state, or the wannabe state, where control is the main goal. Whether or not the control that states seek is benevolent – whether it is for the benefit of democracy or for the benefit of some political, military or industrial interest – is beside the point. Journalism's legitimacy rests on its independence from these interests.

The root causes of the current crisis in journalism are usually identified as economic or a mixture of technological and economic causes. Crisis, in itself, signals disruption, uncertainty and indecision – the lack of confidence in strategies as old, familiar forms dissolve. As the forces disruptive to journalism are largely thought of as external to the field, primarily identified as the internet, the market is often seen as both the source of the crisis and its solution. Indeed, the story that many scholars tell about the current crisis in journalism is one of failed market strategies.

The story begins when the internet arrived in the mid-1990s, changing the way business and communication are conducted. Failure number one in this situation was to give away the news for free (Chyi, 2013). This eroded the two-sided business model where income can be expected from both audiences and advertisers. Then, when the financial crisis hit in 2008, newspaper companies moved to consolidate operations. Because the cost of borrowing rose at the same time, news firms centralized operations, laid off staff, sold buildings or closed down altogether to save money (see Lacy & Sohn, 2011). The second strategic failure was therefore to continue to expect high margins through times of crisis, which in turn hurt the product companies were trying to convince people to buy. As revenues remained lost to new substitutes in the advertising industries, primarily third-party intermediaries such as Facebook, Google and YouTube, companies began to disregard their main product, news, in favor of their secondary product, audiences. Metrics emerged as the new gold in the industry, the capitalization of which relies on corporate resources – technical knowledge, infrastructures and economies of scale.

In this crisis narrative, proposed solutions concerning how to emerge from this disruption have more often been about markets than content. While external commentators are urging news organizations to focus on their main asset – connecting with audiences through quality journalism – industry players tend to focus on securing and expanding their markets. As the industry has lost faith that there may be new audience markets to be found, the effort to secure reader markets leads journalism down a path of segmentation, polarization and politicization. Identifying stable readership segments in the fringes provides more financial predictability than aiming for the middle market, where willingness to pay is low. As classified and retail advertising markets begin to look as if they are lost forever to social media platforms, news organizations move in on the audience metric market. Here, a new competitive arena has emerged in the area of personalization – an area where the global tech giants are already experts. Competitiveness in this arena requires a certain size, infrastructure and skill set, as programmatic advertising is based on big user data and algorithms to sort and use this data. In the two-sided market, then, news companies have given up competing on two fronts. Instead, they seem content to divide audience segments among themselves, where there are still certain revenues to be found in customer loyalty, concentrating instead on winning the battle in the advertising markets. As information is the thing that moves people through the networks of the internet, this may indeed prove to be a sound strategy – capitalizing on the value of journalism as the information environment becomes more precarious, with growing amounts of propaganda and fake news.

Professionalism, authority and boundaries

While news organizations try to move out of this crisis using economic strategies, journalism is not, as Alexander (2016, p. 7) observes, just a market-responsive business; it is also a profession. The elements embedded in this professional dimension refer to journalism's democratic role in society – the social contract of the press that holds journalists responsible for overseeing the state on behalf of the citizenry. This is essentially journalism's main selling point – the claim that a professionalized, expert vocation with established ethics and norms performs a critical function in society on which all other spheres depend. Citizens, states and markets are each served by the free flow of information, laws that guarantee this freedom and rules that regulate its conduct. To maintain the position that this role yields, journalism – in its weak semi-professional status – is in constant need of boundary maintenance.

Professions, according to the sociologist Thomas F. Gieryn (1983), are involved in a continuous struggle for authority, power and resources. Because threats to professionalism primarily amount to a perceived lack of exclusivity and knowledge-based jurisdiction, journalism's permeability – the high level of mobility and the constant competition for entry into the professional definition – means that a lack of exclusivity and monopoly requires significant boundary work. Boundary maintenance involves borders of demarcation: distinguishing the work of members from the practices and products of non-members. These kinds of boundary disputes signal contests for authority, involving the knowledge, methods, values and organizations that separate journalism from non-journalism. As journalism finds itself in a demanding jurisdictional battle – involving contests with anything from fake news to right-wing media, propaganda, processes of capture, commercialization and content marketing – the norms and myths of the institutional dimension of journalism become increasingly important.

Because institutions can be thought of as social practices that are durable across time and space (Giddens, 1984), institutions consist of rules and resources. As agents act within the institution, they invoke the institutional order, making it meaningful by reproducing it through action, referred to as a "logic of appropriateness" (March & Olsen, 1984). The durability of institutions can thus be observed in how context conditions action and in how these conditions are reproduced by individuals engaging in regularized social practice. In the relationship between individuals and institutions, the institutional frame contributes practical reasoning (Hall & Taylor, 1996) – frameworks for expanding patterns of action and reactions that give meaning within the context they occur. When contexts change, however, questions about institutional self-maintenance become crucial.

The direction in institutional theory called new institutionalism is particularly helpful in looking at this situation, as it considers how institutions perform under social and political changes (Scott, 1995). New institutionalism focuses on the multiplicity and flexibility of goals within social systems and considers collectives to be in a reciprocal relationship with their socioeconomic environments. As an institution, journalism is constantly involved in the conflict between economic gain and the struggle for legitimacy (Ryfe, 2006, p. 204). Embedded in the journalistic institution is therefore this constant boundary work, to which the profession has naturally built up an arsenal of defense mechanisms that can be mobilized in the face of disruption, crisis and challenges to authority. These defenses consist of the myths, norms and ideals of the profession embedded in the social contract of the press. Hence, although journalism faces disruption, the rules that guide journalistic production remain relatively stable – communicating the foundations of journalism as an institution of news production.

As boundaries assist in marking the difference between what is news and what is not news, journalists are mobilized in this endeavor. Journalists follow the rules of the institution because they want to be recognized as journalists. Because journalism becomes even more norm-dependent as the complexity of institutions surrounding the field increases, the boundaries of journalistic practice become more pronounced, signaling the difference between real journalism and non-journalism, including fake news, public relations, advertising and editorializing. In this way, regularized practices – fact checking, right of reply and sourcing – serve as countermeasures to the increasing complexities facing the profession (Cook, 1998). When journalists engage in these practices, they confirm the institutional order, demarcating the boundaries between journalism and other fields, such as the political and economic fields. Although the internet both enables and restrains traditional journalistic practices, enduring vocational procedures also largely determine how these resources are utilized and how new rules are formed. This type of border patrol behavior by institutional members circulates norms and myths within the profession to an orthodoxy that helps to create stability within the field, even in the face of a marked disruption.

Crisis, market and civil society

Even though the crisis in journalism, as Rasmus Kleis Nielsen (2016) points out, speaks to several different crises at once rather than a universal one, the market gets the bulk of the blame for this situation. The fact that the market is a reality, though, puts the news economy in a position of pressure. Whether this pressure is seen in a stakeholder light, where the market consists of a number of interlinking processes, practices and strategies, or in a critical light, where creative industries are capitalist institutions involved in the creation of symbolic commodities, the market holds several points of entry for analysis. When journalism is seen as a business, then, we quickly run into issues of control, interest and power, exercised through the mechanisms of the market.

Most of the debates on journalism and its place between the state and the market are nested in the concept of the public sphere – where political life is contrasted with private life, where consumption takes place. The public sphere is often painted as the space between the state and the market (Garnham, 1986). It is where public debate takes place, where battles for hegemony are fought (Raeijmaekers & Maeseele, 2015) through asymmetries of power (Dahlberg, 2007) determined by class (Hallin, 1994, p. 6). This space is, in Habermas' terms (1971), compromised both by private economic interests in the market and by state interests, particularly through the close embeddedness of private citizens into the welfare state (Dawes, 2014).

This space – civil society – is positioned by Ryfe (2017) as one of the forces "pulling" on journalism. Civil society is, in Ryfe's terms, the set of institutions between the state, the economy and the family, orbiting around the state. Ryfe says, however, that journalism does not itself constitute the civil or public sphere. It "never lies completely within one sphere of public life" (p. 43). For one thing, Ryfe says that journalism has a different purpose in civil society than it has in the market. Moreover, to him, professionalism itself should be seen a separate force in the creation of journalism as it emerged between the state, the market and civil society. Hence, in the discussion of what forces influence journalism in the construction of news, researchers tend to emphasize different aspects of the larger structures and processes influencing journalism. Journalism, then, is a civil institution – one among several. Journalism is not the public sphere in itself; it is part of the public sphere. Hence, when we talk about journalism's fundamental problem as its position between the state and the market, we are talking about binary forces that influence and condition journalism. The condition we are talking about here is one of closeness – journalism's movement towards the fields that enable its existence. Civil society or the public sphere legitimizes journalism and its function, but it is not something that journalism can move closer to – certainly not to an extent that may shake its boundaries.

The main difficulty in pinning down these influences is largely geographical. At least in the context of digital disruption, business model disintegration and questions of legacy media sustainability, the geographical dimension is important. Whereas the state is national, the market is global. As analytical variables, these are problematic entities. Communication systems are still largely national, regulated at the state level; political systems are similarly situated. Forces of political or ideological control exist within a defined nation-state context, rarely spilling over into extranational spheres. But whereas journalism's relationship to the state and the polity is a national nexus, its relationship to the market is increasingly global. Advertising and audience markets used to be nationally bound. Now they are potentially global. They are definitely global for the big platform players currently assuming larger and larger shares of national advertising markets. Thus, the media consumer market is global, allowing audiences to access global product markets. The sphere of political influence for journalism, however, is national. Journalism's main products – voters and consumers – now operate in spheres of different sizes. Voters remain nation-bound, tied to a confined market space of political choices. Consumers, and indeed advertisers, operate across state lines, moving in long-tail markets bound only by the imagination.

Theoretical basis and empirical focus

The amount of literature on the relationship between journalism and politics, democracy and the public sphere is considerable, if not absolutely enormous. Although investigations into media democracy, media regulations, political communication and journalism and civic culture add great insight into journalism's relationship with the state, many of these perspectives fail to comprehensively attend to the market. Moreover, these perspectives are largely normative. That is why democratic or political theory is not really all that helpful in our current endeavor. The only theoretical perspective that really considers both states and markets in the constitution of journalism is institutional sociology.

The argument presented in this book is rooted in institutional sociology, resting on three strands of theory related to journalism studies. At the base of this theoretical architecture is Giddens' theory of structuration (1984), where action is possible within the duality of structure. Giddens explains how our ability to act as agents within a larger social structure is dependent on the rules and resources we can access within that structure. As agents, we are to some extent restricted by the structures that surround us, but what we do can also affect their composition. Giddens' vantage point for the theory of structuration is to balance the constraining influence of structure over human action embedded in the established sociological framework. By abandoning "the equation of structure with constraint" (p. 220), Giddens instead bases his theory "on the proposition that structure is always both enabling and constraining, in virtue of the inherent relation between structure and agency" (p. 169). Journalism is shaped by the rules of the structure, but the application of available resources also contributes to maintaining or changing those rules. Here, the sociology of professions explains how professional power is assumed and maintained within the field, including the boundary maintenance (Gieryn, 1983) needed to ensure distance to other fields. New institutionalism is useful here in describing how institutions negotiate social power and field disintegration in periods of complex and fast-moving changes. Institutional sociology thus provides the vantage point for looking at journalism as situated between the state and the market while considering the interplay between fields and retaining some agency to the institution within this position.

Second, to properly understand the relationship between journalism and states and markets, political economic theory offers an entry point that allows for analyses of institutional influences and macro forces, including the mobilization of Marxist ideas about power and change. Although critical political economy (CPE) has a tendency to overemphasize the role of the market in shaping journalism, media systems theory serves to balance this perspective through its focus on the close relationship between politics and the press. Media systems theory, while largely overlooking the economic field that CPE generally accounts for, also seeks more holistic explanations for the function of journalism in society. Thus, the theoretical nexus that constitutes the vantage point for this endeavor consists of the institutional sociology that considers what journalism is, the CPE perspective that considers the role of the market and the media systems perspective that considers the role of politics and the state.

Scandinavia is a good place to study these assumptions. The Nordic media model is, at its core, based on the state/market balance. Media regulations and journalistic professionalism as well as economic and political culture are based on maintaining a balance between the state and the market, ensuring that neither has too much influence over social institutions and individuals. The Nordic context thus provides a good case study for analyzing journalism in the age of disruption, not least because Scandinavian media still foster relationships with both fields and because legacy media largely maintain leading market positions attained during the analog era. Because of the high level of digitalization of these societies, their general wealth and high education levels have allowed global players in the information markets to move in to severely disrupt journalism's business model. Market/state proximities in journalism in Scandinavia therefore have certain expressions – expressions that one may expect to be particularly noticeable, given the mixed system in which these media operate.

These theoretical frameworks and empirical realities will be laid out in the following chapters. Following this general introduction to the problem at hand, Chapter 2 outlines the theoretical basis for placing journalism in a relationship with the state and the market, and Chapter 3 presents the Scandinavian media landscapes according to media systems theory. Chapters 4 and 5 describe journalism's proximity to both state and market. Chapter 6 concludes the book by synthesizing empirical chapters with theory, presenting an overall framework for analyzing the disruptions facing journalism in the digital era and discussing its strengths and weaknesses.

2 Between the state and the market

The state and the market are presented as binary oppositions in journalism studies. Although both are considered profane, to what extent one is more profane than the other depends on context. In some contexts, the market works as an emancipatory force, freeing journalism from the oppressive hand of the state. In other circumstances, the market is seen as corrupting journalism, and the protective hand of the state serves as a shield against commercial forces. In this first narrative, described by Curran (2012) among others, the market not only liberates news media from state censorship and taxation – it also widens the scope of participation, opening up spaces for deliberation and consumption for the marginalized and disenfranchised. In the second narrative, more common than the first (cf. Bagdikian, 2004; McChesney, 2003; McManus, 1994), market forces debase journalism through lowest-common-denominator content, adjusting to advertising and owners' interests – limiting the reach of public deliberation by emphasizing consumption over participation.

The potential benevolence of states and markets in terms of journalism's institutional autonomy thus depends on the system in which journalism is practiced. In the Scandinavian democratic corporatist welfare systems, the state serves as a guarantee of positive rights – rights to information access, freedom of expression and protection of journalists. Here, states regulate media to guard against market failure – the main motivating force for state involvement in ensuring an open and inclusive public sphere. In other systems, such as the market-oriented liberal systems, state intervention should be reserved to the protection of negative rights – ensuring only that freedoms do not impinge on the rights of others. Or in polarized pluralist societies, where economic and political interests often overlap in their influence over the press, money and power can both serve to corrupt journalism.

Markets and states are therefore forces that work on journalism. Journalism's main boundary-maintaining challenge in this pressure situation is to secure its borders of autonomy, necessary to ensure legitimacy in a third sphere of influence: civil society, where its commercial and political "customers" reside. If journalism is perceived to be compromised by either political and economic interests, the press has failed in its democratic mission: to provide people with the information they need to make free and informed decisions in the political marketplace, where votes are the main currency. Although journalism has always been caught in this double pressure, how the institution manages this pressure depends on its institutional strength.

This strength can be provided by both the market and the state. For one thing, rich media organizations are potentially strong media organizations, because a sound financial basis provides editors with the protection necessary for assuming risk – the risk of lawsuits as well as the risk of losing audiences through unpopular reporting. Money, therefore, can be a source of journalistic freedom. Having a strong market position also provides long-term security, as strong brands tend to attract more investments and more serious investors, whose investments are best secured by maintaining a strong brand. The market economy can thus be a safeguard for journalistic freedom and editorial agenda-setting power, and thus a basis for service as a democratic force. But market forces can also weaken journalism. When economies are weak, owners who aim to maintain profit margins can take this out on journalistic resources and push the editorial agenda towards commercial news values, sensationalism and political pandering. Economies of scale also encourage owners to constantly grow their holdings, making ownership more concentrated, pushing media towards monopoly situations. Such negative market effects can be mitigated by state intervention. States can introduce restrictions on ownership concentration, provide support for marginalized, diversifying media and ensure a minimum of journalistic oversight by maintaining systems of public service media. Such state intervention can be used to limit the concentration of money and power in the media system and to provide the financial basis needed to ensure that not all media have to pander to the market. But states can also use their legislative and economic powers to control the media by controlling ownership, access or content, making news media a tool for propaganda.

Journalism is therefore threatened by, and strengthened by, both forces. Maintaining the proper distance to both spheres is therefore central to the autonomy of the journalistic institution. Hence, when the boundaries of the journalistic institution are discussed, the jurisdiction should not be conceptualized simply in relation to its closest rivals, such as the public relations industry, actors in the blogosphere or fake news panderers; it should also be related to the framework conditions that shape the political and economic spheres pressing on the journalistic institution.

Foundations

States and markets are fundamental to the theoretical treatment of journalism's role and position in society. Often, they entail fundamental blocks of influence in questions about democracy, autonomy and critical debate. Habermas (1971), in his treatment of the transformation of the public sphere, positions the public sphere between the realm of the state and the realm of the private. As the public sphere emerged, Habermas contends, private interests separated the press from the state but not from the markets. Although power exists in both realms, ownership concentration and commercial interest turned the public into consumers, which embedded the public sphere too closely to the sphere of the marketplace (cf. Dawes, 2014). An independent, self-regulating media should be autonomous of the political and economic systems in order to serve legitimately as a conduit of public debate.

Foucault (2010) treats this distinction between state and market as fundamental to liberal thought. However, he saw the liberal separation of state and market as compromised by an emergent neoliberalism that adapted market principles to the state. Once market principles begin to condition the interventionist powers of the state, the distinction between citizen and consumer is compromised, cementing social differences. Bourdieu (1984), in turn, sees the state and the market as social fields – social categories where norms and practices form the capital that enable the exercise of power. Adding civil society to the mix, Ryfe (2017) suggests that journalism sits between the social fields that inhabit public life, with each pulling journalism in different directions. "The state pulls in one direction, the market in another, and civil society in still another direction" (p. 13), the outcome of which depends on the makeup of social fields, the strength of forces involved and journalism's ability to push back.

Within this state/market binary, a number of dichotomous concepts illustrate the oppositional pulls that the state and the market exert on journalism as something in between the two. Here, capitalism and democracy constitute oppositional realms; private and public interests are presented as contrary, as is the role of the citizen and the role of the consumer. In the realm of media, public service and commercial media are often dichotomized (Jacka, 2003; McQuail, 1998). Here, the logic of the market is seen as opposite to the needs of the public sphere, to the extent that "good" journalism is dichotomized with market journalism (Ryfe, 2017, p. 128) and entertainment is opposite to information (Lacy & Sohn, 2011). As such, aspects such as commercialism and non-commercialism, democratic and undemocratic, profitable and unprofitable are associated with "good", public service–oriented journalism on the one hand versus "bad", market-driven, commercialized journalism on the other.

In a Western, liberal-democratic context, then, the market is decidedly viewed as worst among the forces pulling on journalism. Although the state is often seen as potentially precarious in terms of limiting the editorial freedom of the press in polarized, authoritarian and liberal systems of governance (cf. Hallin & Mancini, 2004), in democratic corporatist media systems, the state is often viewed as the safeguard for journalistic freedom, professionalism and public service. This is because regulation is often presented as the state's way of securing against market failure (Mosco, 2009, p. 175) – the inability of the market to effectively allocate important goods and services (Taylor, 2007, p. 15; Pickard, 2017, p. 56). According to Victor Pickard (2017), market failure "typically occurs when private enterprise withholds investments in critical social services because it cannot extract the returns that would justify expenditures, or when customers fail to pay for such services' full social benefit" (p. 56). Regulation is therefore an expression of state reaction to problems in the market. Though outright market *failure* is more of a theoretical concept than a reality in most countries, the market is still associated in journalism studies with processes of deregulation, liberalization and privatization – processes that are politically enacted by the state, leading to the concentration of ownership and the commercialization of content.

The market

A market is usually defined in economics as the sphere of economic exchange – a place where commodities are bought and sold, where people meet to exchange goods and services (Meehan & Torre, 2014, p. 62). Such exchanges occur from the mutual interaction and observation of various groups of producers who seek to satisfy consumer tastes. Once consumer tastes constitute a market, producers tailor their products to the popular taste (Peterson & Anand, 2004, p. 317). Media markets could, therefore, be rather diverse markets, as customers have a wide variety of tastes and preferences that a multitude of sellers could seek to satisfy. The concept of "popular taste", however, suggests that there is potentially a mass market. Here, the aim is to satisfy as many people's tastes as possible without needing a costly differentiation of products. This tends to reduce both the number and variety of products in the market, to which the question of diversity and consumer choice becomes pertinent.

The basis of classic market theory is Adam Smith's model of liberal markets. Smith describes how fully free and competitive markets should ideally work to provide economic growth and political stability (as described in Meehan & Torre, 2014, p. 63). Such a market needs a large number of buyers and sellers. Buyers express demands and bargain with sellers, who try to anticipate changes in demand in order to profit. This process should be conducted free of religious, ethical or similar concerns. Moreover, complete information was seen as important to ensure that participants could evaluate their self-interest in transactions. Smith asserted that markets that did not satisfy buyer demand could foster dissatisfaction with the political status quo. Political stability rendered by such markets could largely be assured by governments, particularly by facilitating easy entry and exit to the markets, enabling the large number of buyers and sellers needed to sustain the system. Although Smith failed to safeguard the problem of cooperation between sellers by introducing government regulation, he also saw markets as social institutions that could outperform private, secretive and corrupt forms of power (Garnham, 2014, p. 43). This market utopia has been largely debunked by political economy scholars focusing in particular on distributional conflicts between labor and capital. In reality, as Meehan and Torre (2014, p. 65) explain, the neoliberal economic theory that deregulated markets in the 1980s and 1990s went thoroughly against Smith's ideas, fostering ownership concentration (meaning fewer sellers) and conglomeration (meaning less innovation), leading to incomplete consumer information. Media markets, however, are different from normal commodities markets in that media are also public goods.

Media markets

Media markets are places where media products are circulated. According to McManus (1994), there are four markets for news: the audience market, where news organizations compete for readers and viewers; the stock market, where higher valuation is the goal; the market for sources, where journalists compete for information; and the advertising market, where revenue is the goal. The markets are connected, as higher performance in one – for instance, the audience market – should increase stock prices and strengthen the product, thereby attracting more advertising and more information sources. As media companies seek audiences and advertisers, content and distribution, they also compete with other media.

Media markets are, however, largely shaped by geographic orientation, both in terms of the particular products sold and their distribution (Lacy & Sohn, 2011, p. 160). As such, the size of media markets is determined by the availability of market shares, or the number of buyers, readers or viewers that can be attained. Media markets are also two-sided markets, meaning the news product is sold in two markets: the audience market and the advertising market. Exchanges in media markets therefore involve both the content provided by sellers to consumers for money and potential attention to advertising. Because of this two-sidedness, sellers in media markets compete for consumers' time as well as their money. As such, media markets are information-attention markets. Here, attention is a scarce good. Media markets have therefore been described as "fuzzy" (Lacy, 1993). Demand is uncertain in media markets because the products are changed regularly and new products are constantly introduced. Moreover, understanding consumer demand for news is highly uncertain because the meaning of news is a function of individual perception and content. Risk, therefore – "the potential loss or gain from a decision" (Lacy & Sohn, 2011, p. 160) – is highly characteristic of media markets. This risk is particularly embedded in high costs and unpredictable profits.

The uncertainty that characterizes market environments, uncertainty being "the subjective probability of a decision resulting in the preferred outcome of a decision" (ibid), is generally exacerbated by technological development. The internet, as such, introduced more choice, both to audiences and advertisers. As imperfect but acceptable substitutes for news have proliferated, the internet has also increased the risk of failed market strategies. Whereas media companies have multiple goals where financial and journalistic goals are both present, multiple goals mean companies must prioritize, and such priorities shape strategies. For private media firms facing the digital disruption in the 1990s and 2000s, a common strategy was to cut costs. As companies grew in size, accompanied by increased borrowing costs in the 2000s, firms reacted by laying off staff to secure profits. This led to a merger of newspapers driven by two strategies: to reduce competition and to eradicate unprofitable markets, primarily here in the fringes of content and geographical markets.

It is within this context of the market nature of journalism that terms such as *marketization*, *commercialization* and *market logic* are usually mobilized. As "the forces of disruption have arrived in journalism from outside the field, and have come primarily from the market" (Ryfe, 2017, p. 137), we now have a situation where, as Nechushtai (2018) notes, the media are "market-based but no longer profitable" (p. 194). There is largely a critical tone embedded in these tales of the effects of digital disruption on journalism. The market is seen as a force pushing the strategies of media companies towards sustaining the commercial aspect of news operations over sustaining the democratic or public role of journalism. In this narrative of crisis and disruptive innovation, where the unsustainability of journalism's business model becomes apparent, the common conception that underlies the current state/market problem that journalism faces is that news media will only serve democracy if it is profitable to do so (McChesney, 2004).

The logic of the market

Market forces are largely blamed for the problems facing journalism. On the one hand, the market is a force working on journalism. On the other, market forces also involve a logic that news organizations assume in order to face disruption – to solve its problems. So, what exactly are market forces? And how do they lead to market logic? The basic market force is profit – increasing returns. This is the basic idea of capitalism: constant growth. Other forces in the market are demand and supply – what people want to buy, and what is for sale. Competition for buyers drives company strategies, as do the profits and losses resulting from these exchange activities. In media markets, the main resource that drives strategy is the scarce good that is people's attention.

The term *force* is used to describe a variety of aspects that impact on the organized production of news. Such forces can involve a number of things – such as commercialization or disruption – that are assumed to have a negative impact on journalism. But the forces working on journalism go beyond purely economic forces. Indeed, market forces are but one of many pressures influencing production in the media sector. Peterson and Anand (2004) identify six forces that shape the cultural output of the creative industries: technology, laws and regulations, the industry structure, the organizational structure, occupational careers and the market. Laws and regulations constitute the rules by which fields develop, but industrial fields also tend to gather around new technologies that in turn shape legal frameworks and markets. Organizational structures shape labor and authority systems, and industry structures inform levels of innovation and standardizations in the market. The market, in turn, shapes actors' attempts to satisfy consumer demands. These forces are reflected in McQuail's (2003, pp. 6–7) list of factors that affect journalistic conduct and performance, in which he includes the legal and regulatory system; structures of ownership and control; general organizational features and routines; links between media and politics; and market forces, practices and pressures. Market forces, therefore, are among the structures shaping the profession but are also limited in their influence on journalism, to the extent that market pressures compete with other pressures in shaping journalism. We should therefore be specific when discussing exactly what market forces mean in the context of journalism and be specific about how they affect the news industries.

In this context, Meehan and Torre (2014) define a market as "an economic construct that emerges from a combination of legal strictures, economic relationships between entities capable of engaging in transactions, and the structures resulting from those elements that may become institutionalized within an economy over time" (p. 65). To Meehan and Torre (pp. 65–69), markets are themselves constructed through human action in the economic and political spheres. For one thing, laws regulate and criminalize certain trades and behaviors. Actors in the market may, however, try to change these rules towards a framework that is more favorable to them. Furthermore, they recognize that the relations of power and control that affect production, distribution and consumption are often unequal. Markets also become institutionalized, as persistent structures of markets set the parameters for entry to, action within and exit from the market. Nevertheless, institutional markets also involve oversight, often by government entities assuming market protecting functions. Hence, whereas the market may be a force affecting journalism negatively (e.g. Christians et al., 2009; Entman, 2005), the market itself is influenced by the structures surrounding it, the agents operating within it and the rules and resources at their disposal.

Market logic, however, is generally used to denote processes of domination, control and profit. In this context, market logic tends to entail mass-market expansion and maximization of consumption through economies of scale forged by worldwide media giants that aim to increase their potential political, cultural and gatekeeping powers. Market logic in a media industries context therefore also signifies processes of convergence, concentration and globalization, the effects of which lead to hyper-commercialism, trivialization and tabloidization of mass media content. For news media, an orientation towards this market logic "describes how closely a news organization follows market principles" (Ferrucci, 2018, p. 425), meaning audience and profit maximization. Market-oriented news content, as such, operates "within the parameters of profitability" (Baldasty, 1992, p. 140). According to Beam (2001), "a strong market orientation implies that an organization's long-run success depends on identifying and fulfilling customers' informational wants and needs" (p. 467), shifting away from a professional decision-making model. From an organizational perspective, such an orientation affects the content, routines and perceptions of journalists (Shoemaker, Vos & Reese, 2009).

While all media are market-oriented to a degree – this is a continuum rather than an either/or – market orientation is one way to deal with uncertainty. As such, as uncertainty rises, market orientation increases. This process usually involves heightened attention to market research, the aim of which is to understand how to meet the needs of potential customers, to create a better fit with the environment and improve performance (Beam, 2001). Although public interests are usually seen as being at odds with this market-oriented model, certain content created just to make money (Baldasty, 1992) has also been heralded as democratizing – enlarging the sphere of public concern (e.g. Meijer, 2001), including marginal audiences, and expanding citizens' rights to the consumer sphere. Therefore, while definitions of market journalism "carry an implicit assumption that markets, by definition, result in lower-quality journalism" (Lacy & Sohn, 2011, p. 159), profit can also work as a force that drives diversity in the products offered and audiences served.

For journalism as a profession and for news as an organizational mode of production, the ability to attract income from advertising and sustain or preferably increase share value also involves a long line of thinking that aims to shield journalism from the market. The market, in this sense, says Ryfe (2017), forms "the necessary background against which other ideals are put forward in the field" (p. 129) – ideas such as truth, community and democracy. "Cast as an ever-present threat, [the market therefore] animates and catalyzes journalists every bit as much as their more positive ideals" (p. 129). As every hero needs a villain, journalism also uses the potential corruption of the market as a backdrop for ideological boundary maintenance, professional celebration and differentiation within the field.

Neoliberalism: the great culprit

Cast as the main force that drives journalism towards the market logic is the political process of neoliberalism. Simultaneously seen as the antithesis to liberalism and the bane of high modernism (Hallin, 1994), the state and the market are, as opposites, tied to the dichotomies born of neoliberalism's entry into postwar politics – of modernity (good) and postmodernity (bad), citizen (good) and consumer (bad), universal rationality (good) and discursive particularity (bad), information (good) and entertainment (bad), public service (good) and commercial media (bad). Indeed, neoliberalism is in many ways synonymous with the logic of the market, as it embodies, for the media at least, a shift in regulatory framework from cultural to market policy, involving privatization of public assets, liberalization of competition to include more players (McChesney, 2007, p. 177), deregulation of economic sectors and corporatization of state media. Not only does neoliberalism assume the principles of the market for the state (Davies, 2013, p. 33), it also draws in the boundaries of the state (Lunt & Livingstone, 2012, p. 20), extending the reach of market mechanisms. But more than that, says Dawes (2014), "neoliberalism cannot be reduced to the passing of power from the state to the market, [it] involves the changing governmental relation *between* the state and market, and *between* citizens and consumers" (p. 702), undermining citizenship and the public sphere. To that extent, neoliberalism removes the very necessity of distinguishing between politics and economy, or between citizens and consumers (Foucault, 2010; Murdock, 1993).

The movement from modernity to postmodernity entails a shift from the stability of state and market towards fragmentation and disruption where consumer and citizen identities become blurred. Media institutions in turn become an instrument of the market, as communication networks are key to control and coordination of production, distribution and consumption, particularly through the "serialization" of cultural production, the commodification of ideas and providing the primary site for advertising (Murdock, 1993). To this end, the neoliberal leviathan is a monster largely mobilized by critical political economists. More than reflecting trends towards commercialism, however, neoliberalism in a journalism context is more fruitfully tied to what Hallin (1994) refers to as the passing of high modernism in American journalism. Transforming journalism on two fronts, the passing of high modernism explains how journalism's increasing distance from the state, and its increasing closeness to the market, negatively affected political journalism in the United States. Here, journalism's political insulation, being part of the political establishment while also being able to criticize it, became disentangled at the same time as its economic insulation fortified. Whereas distance from the economic sphere was coupled with proximity to the political sphere, the passing of high modernism signals a shift in journalism's state/market relations – becoming embedded in the economic sphere while being increasingly pushed away from the political sphere. Thus, the context within which journalism is practiced is also dependent on the push/pull relationship between the state and the market.

Liberalism vs. welfare capitalism

The tidal wave of neoliberalism has not hit all media systems equally. Scandinavian economic systems are more characterized by welfare capitalism (Esping-Andersen, 1990) – a system that is often contrasted with liberal market economics (Iversen & Stephens, 2008). A fundamental dilemma in reconciling democratic and capitalist goals is that while the former is based on an egalitarian power principle (one person, one vote), the latter produces inequalities of property and income. The varieties of capitalism approach removes the dichotomized relationship between the state and the market and replaces it with an institutional approach where market institutions are designed to aid agents in making the best use of their productive assets (Iversen, 2006, p. 614, citing Hall & Soskice, 2001). Hence, economic institutions have to be understood in relation to other institutions. As such, the welfare state is linked to the economy in a way that creates beneficial complementarities. Here, companies that are exposed to risk will favor a social insurance system, provided and ensured by the state. The state can also offer protection to industry that can safeguard growth, not just provide hindrances. Welfare capitalism is therefore characterized by mutual dependencies within the system, connecting economic performance to the type of human capital that states can engender in cooperation between political parties, unions and the owners of production (Iversen & Stephens, 2008). Markets, therefore, are a "mixed bag of institutions", some that increase efficiency and some that decrease efficiency (North, 1990, p. 69).

There is, therefore, some discrepancy between the narratives of state/market relations in theories about journalism and the complexity afforded to the relationship in institutional theories. In Curran's (2005) outline of the liberal narrative of media history, media is presented as "an agency of information and debate that facilitates the functioning of democracy" (p. 129). Here, the role of media in informing the electorate, serving as a channel of communication between the people and its rulers and providing a forum for debate "can best be achieved [. . .] through the free market" (p. 129). The problem with the market, Curran points out, is that many of its features tend to undermine debate, including high barriers to entry, information divides and simplification. Habermas (1994) was also at odds with the idea that a liberal model provides the best conduit for democracy. Habermas contrasted liberalism, where politics is the expression of an aggregate of individual wills acting in self-interest, with republicanism's adherence to consensus and common-good principles in democratic will-formation. The reduction, however, of the market and market forces to the liberal ideology largely obscures the role that the market plays in journalism. Although it is true that economies of scale and scope can lead to homogenization and concentration, actors who chose to play outside market rules, such as radical and collectivist media, can also find niches in such marketplaces (cf. Christians et al., 2009, p. 133). States also usually operate with a number of exceptions to market principles, allowing state intervention in markets based on exemptions (e.g. art galleries), externalities (e.g. regulating pollution), and exceptions (typically during crisis; Davies, 2013).

More than reflecting actual differences, the particularities of democratic systems and the journalistic roles that correspond to them are not as important in practice as they are in theory. The criticisms of the liberal system in many ways reflect more the differences in scholarly approaches within the field of journalism studies than philosophical and ontological boundaries between journalistic professionalisms and institutions in different countries. To what extent the free press ideal, the watchdog ideal or the fourth estate ideal belong to the liberal tradition or not and to what extent liberal press narratives are mobilized outside of liberal-democratic systems are beside the point. What matters are the differences implied by the various structures imbued by different democratic systems and the framework that the state/market relationship in various systems imply for journalism.

The state

States are primarily defined by territory and legality. Moreover, states are thought of as political entities – self-governing and organized political communities under one government. Classic sovereignty theory holds that states have a central authority with unrestricted ruling power to make and enforce the law and that this power holds primacy over all other powers. Liberal-democratic state systems are predominant in what is often termed the Western world – developed, institutionalized, urbanized, capitalist, secular and modern societies, where the accountability and legitimacy of political authority is characterized by democratic standards and citizen rights. Essentially, in liberal democracies, political elites derive their power from the support of the demos. The legitimacy of the state must also be sought externally, however, submitting to monitoring and surveillance under international law, managed by supranational authorities such as the U.N. or the E.U. (Held, 2002).

The relationship between journalism and the state has been thoroughly theorized, most notably through media systems theories (see Chapter 3). In Western states, journalism finds its purpose and legitimacy through the state relationship. Journalism sees itself as a cornerstone of the nation state (Zelizer, 2004, p. 112), pinned to the idea of democracy (Curran, 2005, p. 138) yet detached from the state's power (Christians et al., 2009, p. 150). Freedom and responsibility in this relationship go hand in hand. As Schudson (2011) remarks, "News has little to do with political democracy unless the state includes or tolerates a degree of self-government and criticism of state power" (p. 188). Because journalists "consider it their work to inform people so that they can carry out their democratic responsibilities" (Gans, 2003, p. IX), the press must be free from government control because democracy requires informed citizens.

Although the intimate link between journalism and democracy is universally assumed, the question of whether it is possible to have journalism without democracy (Carey, 1989) has been challenged (Schudson, 2008, p. 11, 2011, p. 189). To that end, there are many attempts to classify and model journalism's relationship with democracy. This is not only because there are varieties of democratic forms where journalism assumes different functions, but also because the press "always takes on the form and coloration of the social and political structures within which it operates" (Siebert, Peterson, & Schramm, 1956, p. 1). Moreover, liberal democracy is often taken as a starting point in these attempts (e.g. Christians et al., 2009; Curran, 2005), contrasting the liberal-aggregative model (cf. Raeijmaekers & Maeseele, 2015) with other models such as deliberative democracy (Habermas, 1994), social democracy (Lunt & Livingstone, 2012), welfare democracy (Esping-Andersen, 1990) or agonistic democracy (Mouffe, 2000). The roles or functions that journalism performs within these systems reflect the many forms that the press–state relationship can assume. Regardless of how journalism's function is modeled in relation to state systems, the political culture of a country is thought to shape journalism's relationship with the state, the market and civil society.

State/market and the civil sphere

Overall, the state and the market are oppositional forces pulling on journalism. In Western-focused journalism research, the market is most often posed as a negative force – pulling journalism towards commercialization, homogenization and ownership concentration. The effects of the market pull are thus that journalism is drawn more and more towards the type of content that most noticeably satisfies the largest consumer demand, such as entertainment, sports and consumer issues; that more producers crowd together around the most visible consumer market, making news look more similar across organizations; and that owners seek to concentrate assets to benefit from scale and scope. The role of the state in welfare democracies is to keep the media tethered to the ideals of universalism, free speech and diversity. Welfare states thus regulate media markets to avoid the kind of market failure where journalism ends up underproducing the kind of information that citizens need to make informed decisions as an electorate. To that end, the news media also perform a function for citizens, placing journalism within the context of the public sphere – a space designated between the market and the state (Garnham, 1986, pp. 39–40).

The civil sphere is largely painted as independent of both the market and the state (Thompson, 1995, p. 238), situated between the formal and informal systems of political deliberation (Habermas, 2009, p. 159; cited in Larsen, 2016) – "the set of institutions fitting between the family, the state, and the economy" (Ryfe, 2017, p. 25). Civil society, as such, is a society 'civilized' by the state (Holmes, 1990, p. 22). The potential of the public sphere in liberal-democratic theory is that people acting within the spheres of civil society can form political associations (Ryfe, 2017). In order for this process to occur, free enterprise and freedom of expression are essential. Because early liberal thinkers saw state power as the main threat to individual freedom (Thompson, 1995, p. 238), the civil sphere needed to be free from state intervention, driven instead by the principles of free enterprise. Habermas, however, argued that the potential of the market to support a public sphere was undermined by market logic, primarily the rise of press barons, public opinion manipulation by private interests and the consumerism of citizens. The fall of the public sphere, as it were, was in Habermas' portrayal the effect of not separating the public sphere sufficiently from the market (in Dawes, 2014). In other words, says Dawes,

> the liberal equation of the free press with the free market simultaneously enabled and undermined the public sphere by making the public free from the state but defenseless against the market, frustrating the extent to which they could act as citizens rather than as consumers.
>
> (p. 707)

The public sphere is thus idealized as a space of reasoned and reflexive communication enabling diverse voices discussing public issues (Hallin, 1994) – a space that is compromised by asymmetries of power, inequality in access, corporate domination and censorship and surveillance (Dahlberg, 2007, pp. 827–829). Although journalism is thought to have a central place within this sphere, there is a question, in Hallin's (1994, p. 15) view, whether journalists are part of, or outside of, civil society and to what extent the news media constitute the public sphere. To that end, it is hard to establish to what degree journalism sits within the civil sphere or outside it. In Ryfe's (2017) conception, "journalism emerges in the friction caused by the push and pull of the state, the economy, civil society, and the budding profession" (p. 160). These mechanisms largely describe how institutions interact and engage with each other. As such, says Ryfe, the outcome of the push and pull experienced by journalism from the state, market and civil society depends on the makeup of the social fields that these constitute and journalism's ability to push back against various pressures – the strength of the journalistic institution.

Balance of power

The relationship between the state and the market is a question of the balance of power between the two and the extent to which the state, being the legal and therefore theoretically stronger part, assumes market theory or market logic into its operations. This is a particularly pressing question in social democratic welfare state societies such as in Scandinavia, where policies are guided by principles of universality and the public good rather than market efficiency. Criticism of the so-called neoliberal turn in European politics since the 1980s has painted the power balance as something shifting from the state to the market, notably by the hands of the states themselves. This entails shifts in the relationships between the state and the market and between the concept of citizen and consumer. In media terms, this shift entails moving policy concerns from a realm in which policy is adjusted to the welfare of people as citizens to one in which policy is adjusted to people as consumers. The difference here, says Dawes (2014), is that "the former are assumed to be active members of a political community and the latter the self-interested individuals of civil society" (p. 703).

However, it is important to see the state/market relationship and journalism in conjunction. Historically, the three have been mutually dependent. The modern state developed hand in hand with the market economy. The rise of the modern professions and institutions depended on both to thrive (Thompson, 1995, p. 250). Private property rights as well as freedom of expression were essential ingredients in setting up news organizations in modern industrial societies. But while markets were important for journalism to emerge, journalism also first developed as an occupational field in states where governments allowed it to do so, notably in the United States and the United Kingdom (Ryfe, 2017, p. 162). From these state-rendered conditions, however, journalism was also dependent on the economic field to fortify and grow. In particular, the forces of industrialization and commercialization were needed to turn journalism into an organized mode of production from which an autonomous profession could emerge. News, as it were, did not emerge from interests in improving democracy but from economic interests: in responding to readers seeking diversion, in reporters making careers and in owners searching for profit. Hence, the spheres of the state and the market were both important in enabling the development of modern journalism.

3 The Scandinavian media system

Understanding the relationship between journalism and the state and the market in Scandinavia requires an understanding of the media systems under which journalism operates. Media systems are, in essence, frameworks for understanding the flow of influence between media systems, political systems and economic systems (Ostini & Ostini, 2002). In Hallin and Mancini's (2004) "most similar systems" design, the relationship between media systems and political systems is approached as an effort to establish commonalities based on system characteristics. This aim was first mobilized in an attempt by Siebert et al. (1956) to show how media systems are rooted in differences in political and economic structures. Although media systems are neither uniform nor static, path dependency theory still assumes that the past has a powerful influence on institutional evolution. Media systems analysis therefore entails the empirical analysis of the historical development of institutions within particular circumstances, including their patterns of relationships with other institutions. Unlocking the systematic as well as the problematic aspects of journalism's position within the state/market dichotomy therefore requires that we survey the landscape within which these dynamics play out. As such, this analysis rests on media systems theory and methodology – the aim of which is to understand the dynamics of market and state mechanisms in shaping journalism.

Media systems

The concept of a system is based on the assumption that the parts that make up this system are involved in necessary and dependent relationships (Hardy, 2008, p. 6). Although the idea of systems, rooted in structural functionalism, has been criticized for being too deterministic in outlining relationships of dependency and stability (Flew & Waisbord, 2015), systems also contain principles that help explain other elements in the system, where the interdependence between major actors is defined by competition over resources and positions (Chadwick, 2017, p. 17). As such, media systems research can help unlock common factors shaping developments, establish functions that produce differences, and make connections that explain similarities.

A media system comprises media that are organized within a given society and political system, usually a state (Hardy, 2008, p. 5). The media system under which journalism operates thus entails the political, economic, professional and regulatory forces that shape journalism. Media systems can therefore be thought of as "repositories of historically shaped institutional constraints" (Benson, Blach-Ørsten, Powers, Willig, & Zambrano, 2012, p. 24), or framework conditions that have developed over time to enable journalism as a profession and as a business. Although the methodological nationalism that holds the nation state as the boundary of analysis has been criticized (Couldry & Hepp, 2012; Livingstone, 2012), nation states still remain critical in shaping media policy (Flew & Waisbord, 2015). This pertains in particular to regulation, bound to the vertical links between governments and the organization of major public communications established in the analog era, such as postal services and broadcasting licenses. The nation-state unit of analysis may downplay the role that global networks, global activism and metropolitanism play in the media landscape (Flew & Waisbord, 2015, p. 622); however, most dominant players in most nations are still national in reach. Moreover, nation states remain critical in shaping the organization of media industries and markets (Hardy, 2008, p. 21).

In addition to this methodological nationalism, media systems approaches have been criticized for being stuck in the analog era. Media systems largely assume that national media systems are made up of structures of mass communication – television, radio, newspapers, cinemas etc. (e.g. Hardy, 2012; Pfetsch & Esser, 2012; Syvertsen, Mjøs, Moe, & Enli, 2014). Scholars have particularly noted the lack of consideration for the role of the internet in Hallin & Mancini's media systems framework, something they also acknowledge themselves (2012, p. 289). However, although systems are constantly evolving, developments are always path-dependent – shaped by prior conditions (Hallin & Mancini, 2004). Emerging *hybrid* media systems (Chadwick, 2017), then, are based on the interactions between old logic and new logic. The technologies, norms, behaviors and organizational forms surrounding the media are continually re-created by social actors adapting to the norms and practices of emerging networks to gain advantages. But whereas the internet may indeed impact the conditions under which journalism operates, the main factors assumed to influence media systems are structural, mainly systems of government and their economic, political and cultural subsystems. This creates a problematic disconnect, as nation states have had little power in regulating the activities of global players on national scenes, such as Facebook and Google.

Media systems research is normatively oriented, often with a Western view of democracy, mainly from a U.S. or U.K. vantage point. Most research also assumes that influence flows in one direction from social forces to the media, overlooking how the media may itself impact on the structure (Hardy, 2008, p. 12). Moreover, media systems theories have, on the whole, been criticized for not considering the role of economic influence in media systems (Ostini & Ostini, 2002). When analyzing how journalism faces digital disruption, global competition, failing revenues and news-avoiding audiences, a systems approach allows for a holistic perspective, where agency must be given to journalism as an institution, and to the economic sphere, as much as it is assumed to reside with state legislatures.

Media systems taxonomies

The quote that is usually referenced in this context is from Siebert and colleagues' (1956) original work *Four Theories of the Press*, where it is assumed that "the press always takes on the form and coloration of the social and political structures within which it operates" (p. 1). *Four Theories of the Press* outlined the characteristics of four different media systems, defined largely by geography and political history. Authoritarian media systems were characterized by strong intervention, determined by the absolute power of the state. Libertarian media systems were defined by the absence of state intervention. Here, democracy required only that states were prevented from interfering in people's communication. Privately owned media would mobilize public opinion, serving as a counterweight to state power (Hallin, 1994, p. 3). The American social responsibility system carried a strong democratic ideal towards the role of the press. The 1947 Hutchins Commission was instrumental in the U.S. media systems framework, which argued for state intervention to ensure public service. The Soviet-totalitarian system was grounded in Marxist-Leninist thought, where the press was a carrier of state ideology.

In these early media systems theories, press ownership and the degree of state intervention were central to defining the characteristics that separated media systems. *Four Theories* represents elite power models, where influence flows two ways, between government and the press (Ostini & Ostini, 2002). This press–state relationship approach is recognizable in most subsequent taxonomies of media systems. Altschull (1984), in this context, saw the press as agents of those who would exercise political and economic power, noting that "the content of the news media inevitably reflects the interests of those who pay the bills" (1997, p. 259). Ostini and Ostini (2002) thus criticize early media systems approaches for failing to account sufficiently for the role of the economy in understanding these press systems.

They also note the lack of consideration for the role that journalistic professionalism plays. This role is recognized by Christians et al. (2009, p. 16), who relate different versions of media roles to models of democracy and normative media systems theories. Here, the corporatist tradition is linked to administrative politics, liberal-pluralist democracy and monitorial media. Governments and their economic, political and cultural subsystems thus put different kinds of restraints on the press, depending on the kind of political system under discussion. Their taxonomy reflects the rather standard division of state systems found in media systems theories, distinguishing between capitalist, socialist, democratic or authoritarian systems. Picard (1985) added to the framework a social democratic model to justify public intervention, recognizing social welfare traditions in Europe. Curran (2011) zooms in in on the media in this regard, describing media systems as either public service, dual or market systems. Hence, media systems taxonomies are based on the varying effects that different economic and political systems have on the media. From these taxonomies, media systems research moved beyond normative theory towards identifying variables that shape the relation between media and politics (Flew & Waisbord, 2015).

Hallin and Mancini's (2004) media systems theory represents the most mobilized framework in current media systems research. The aim here is to describe variations in the structure and political role of the media, focusing on the relationship between media systems and political systems. Based on a most similar systems design, and following path dependency theory (North, 1990), their goal is to illustrate how media models are rooted in differences in political and economic structures. To understand media systems, they say, we must understand the social structure of the society in question, including the state system, political parties, civil society developments and the relationship between political and economic interests. In particular, they emphasize the close relationship between the media and the political world, leading them to assume that media systems are rooted in the institutions of the nation state.

Their comparative method entails empirical analysis of the historical development of institutions within particular circumstances, including their patterns of relationships with other institutions. They propose four dimensions by which to compare media systems: the development of media markets, in particular the mass circulation press; political parallelism – that is, the association between media and political parties, or the extent to which the media system reflects major political divisions in society; the development of journalistic professionalism; and the degree and nature of state intervention in the media. A number of variables in political systems account for differences: the constitution of markets, the role of the state, the dominant forms of democracy and pluralism, rational-legal authority and clientelism levels and historical roots. This taxonomy outlines three ideal types of media and politics in Western countries: a liberal system centered on commercial media and characterized by closeness to the economic system, where market forces are dominant; a polarized pluralist system characterized by closeness between media and political interests, where political forces are dominant; and a democratic corporatist system characterized by the close association between media and organized interests, including strong state involvement, where professional forces are dominant.

Hallin and Mancini found that the changes in media systems in their 2004 study could be attributed to commercialization and globalization, leading to a convergence of systems. This led them to observe (rather than hypothesize, as they note in several later publications, e.g. 2012) that Western media systems may be converging towards the liberal model. This observation that media systems are commercializing is linked to developments in the political, economic and civic spheres, particularly the decline of mass parties, the rise of the European common market and increasing European integration (Hallin & Mancini, 2012). Although they also observe the rise of media-centered forms of political mobilization, the convergence towards polarized pluralism (rather than liberalism) is rather understated. This has been observed by other scholars, though, including Brüggemann, Engesser, Büchel, Humprecht, and Castro (2014) in Europe, Nechushtai (2018) in the United States, and Hjarvard (2007) in Denmark. Here, a mixture of market and political forces can be seen as pushing media towards more pronounced or segmented press systems. As Nechushtai observes, the loss of commercial grounding in the advertising market in the U.S. media system is shifting American journalism away from the economic field and towards the political. Greater competition leads to greater differentiation, thus enhancing the emphasis on political nuances (Powers & Benson, 2014). These "market failures" challenge the categorization of the U.S. media system as strictly liberal, says Nechushtai (2018), as they question the notion of keeping governments out of media markets. Intervention is here noted as a possible reaction to a loss of professionalism in U.S. journalism. Nechushtai therefore notes a likely convergence in the U.S. media system towards a mixed model: "independent but politically identified, professional but deskilled and increasingly open to nonprofessionals" (p. 194).

As a method

The variables used in media systems analysis have been problematized, questioned and adjusted (Humphreys, 2012; Norris, 2009). Studies using the Hallin and Mancini framework tend to be designed as case studies, operationalized quantitatively and directed towards questions about political parallelism (Hallin & Mancini, 2017). In this context, Nechushtai (2018) notes that Hallin and Mancini never specified what may constitute high or low values for the variables in their design, making it difficult to qualify what may constitute higher or lower degrees of parallelism, pluralism, clientelism or state intervention in media systems. Hallin and Mancini have nevertheless noted (2012, p. 287) that the four dimensions of their taxonomy (market development, political parallelism, journalistic professionalism and state intervention) probably "travel" better than their three ideal types (liberal, democratic corporatist or polarized pluralist), meaning that their comparative variables should withstand changes and be operationalizable across systems and comparisons.

For our purposes, then, Hallin and Mancini's typology fits well in a research design looking to analyze how the state and the market influence journalism. This is because, say Ostini & Ostini (2002), analyzing the state and the economy should be the first step in media systems analysis. This would imply the following:

(1) Looking at the structure of media markets and paying close attention to the role of the market in changes to the inclusiveness, reach or circulation of the press.
(2) Analyzing political parallelism, or the relationship between the media and the political sphere, tracing developments towards a more polarized or segmented press system.
(3) The state of journalistic professionalism, or the extent to which journalism as an institution withstands increasing pressures from the economic and political spheres.
(4) The degree and nature of state intervention in the media; that is, questioning the positive and negative implications of media regulation.

Using these variables can help identify patterns of media system development and structure (Hallin & Mancini, 2012, p. 300). When it comes to questions about how journalism changes within a media systems context, however, studies have also highlighted how technology serves as a conduit to change (Benson et al., 2012, p. 33). Moreover, journalism's relationship with the economic sphere needs to be put on a more equal footing with the political sphere to enable us to grasp the challenges facing journalism. Not only have the forms and combinations of media company funding been shown to be important in establishing external pluralism in media systems (Benson, 2016; Powers & Benson, 2014), but levels of advertising dependence have also played a part here.

Hallin and Mancini's four dimensions nevertheless remain relevant in analyzing media systems. Although operationalizations of media systems analysis tend to develop more detail into this design (e.g. Brüggemann et al., 2014), which variables are mobilized depends on the object of study and the research questions posed – whether we are looking at relationships between journalism and other sectors of society or whether we are investigating changes to journalism, news or professionalism. Whereas Hallin and Mancini stressed newspaper readership as a fundamental difference between media systems, observing systematic differences in countries where the press developed in mass culture or as part of elite culture (2012, p. 288), Brüggemann and colleagues (2014) emphasize "reach", or the inclusiveness of press markets. These authors also differentiate further the role of the state in the media, separating state involvement into three dimensions: public broadcasting, press subsidies and media ownership regulation. By fine-tuning operationalizations, Brüggemann and colleagues managed to differentiate within the democratic corporatist model, arriving at a northern cluster, a central cluster and a western cluster. The aim in subsequent sections is to analyze the features of the media systems of three countries of this northern cluster: the Scandinavian countries of Denmark, Norway and Sweden.

The Scandinavian media system

Scandinavia is a region of approximately 20 million inhabitants, located in the north of Europe, comprising Denmark, Norway and Sweden. These three countries are highly similar in cultural history, language and political system, and they are considered among the world's most developed democracies. Their media systems fall under Hallin and Mancini's democratic corporatist systems, part of a northern cluster (Brüggemann et al., 2014), identified more specifically as media welfare states (Syvertsen et al., 2014). The characteristics of Western (Hardy, 2008), democratic corporatist (Hallin & Mancini, 2004), Nordic (Syvertsen et al., 2014) or Scandinavian (Allern & Ørsten, 2011; Allern & Pollack, 2017; Lund & Berg, 2009) media systems have been thoroughly described in the literature. The aim in this analysis is to examine the system characteristics in Hallin and Mancini's four dimensions, forming a baseline from which to examine the state/market impact on journalism in the region.

The Scandinavian countries are recognized as different from other democratic corporatist countries in northern Europe, particularly in their political systems. These countries have strong welfare state systems, with mixed economies with strong public elements (Syvertsen et al., 2014). Welfare states emphasize the democratic and participatory aspects of citizenship, are based on redistribution of wealth and aim towards social security (Esping-Andersen, 1990), for which market intervention is the main political tool (Kammer, 2016, p. 143). Social democratic welfare systems like the Scandinavian ones are based on principles of universality, meaning that all citizens are equally entitled to its services and benefits. The principle of universality is thus intent on emancipating the individual from the negative consequences of market and class mechanisms (Esping-Andersen, 1990). Comparatively high taxation levels are necessary to fund these societies, as social security requires a large public sector.

Common features of the Scandinavian political systems include strong rational-legal authority with established rules and procedures and professional civil service guided by public interest. Their political and economic systems are characterized by many small corporations with local affiliations, strong bourgeoisies and established democratic cultures (Ihlen, Skogerbø, & Allern, 2015). Scandinavian politics is predominantly consensus-seeking (Hjarvard & Kammer, 2015), based on voluntarism and institutional contacts between the state and organized interests. Social groups are formally integrated into political processes through a concentrated and centralized interest group system, and solutions are attained through informal coordination and bargaining between groups, state bureaucracies and political parties. Collaboration at such an elite level entails influence beyond the election channel, which obliges organizations towards cooperation. This type of corporate culture implies low levels of political conflict (Ihlen et al., 2015), but politics is more centralized in Denmark and Sweden than in Norway, where center-periphery conflicts are stronger, explained largely by differences in demographic, geographical and political structures. High levels of state intervention mean that Scandinavian governments are active in structuring the public sphere. Public support exists for all central realms of public life, including the media, arts and culture, research and higher education, volunteer organizations and religious communities. Government support is non-political, aimed at ensuring universal, inclusive and diverse public-good structures, the administration of which is guided by the arm's-length principle (Engelstad, Larsen, & Rogstad, 2017). This entails systems of self-governance and self-regulation, meaning organizations can criticize the state and still get support.

Scandinavian countries are intent on sustaining mixed media systems (Regjeringen, 2017). A mixed media system in this context entails the coexistence of a public media sector with high legitimacy alongside successful commercial media. State intervention in media markets to ensure this system includes laws to protect independent editorial functions; oversight systems to oversee that laws and regulations are followed and upheld, and direct and indirect public funding to sustain external diversity at a media systems level. Public service broadcasting and certain parts of the press structure (e.g. local and niche newspapers) receive direct funding, and news organizations are also exempt from VAT. Oversight systems regulate ownership concentration and competition; journalism ethics is overseen by independent professional bodies. Although the state is generally interventionist in its relation to the media, there are also limits to state power, primarily in the form of strong legal protections for journalism – protecting free speech, editorial freedom, information access and right of reply.

Syvertsen and colleagues (2014) thus describe the organization of Nordic media systems (including Denmark, Finland, Iceland, Norway and Sweden) as resting on four pillars: universal services, editorial freedom, cultural policy and consensus media policies. This means that communication services are organized as public goods, editorial freedom is institutionalized, cultural media policies include content obligations to sustain diversity and quality and cooperation exists between stakeholders. Because these features also reflect the organized welfare state characteristics of other socioeconomic and political institutions in the Nordic region, the authors come to describe the Nordic countries as media welfare states. This system evolved during the analog era. Principles of continuity have had path-dependent media policy effects, largely sustaining established media structures. State support has, in particular, helped maintain local newspaper structures and high newspaper readership, distinguishing the Nordic newspaper markets from the rest of Europe. Publicly funded broadcasting also helped sustain mass audiences when deregulation in the 1980s and 1990s introduced more competition into broadcasting markets, the reaction to which included licensing commercial public service broadcasting – creating characteristic "duopolies" in the broadcasting markets (Lund & Berg, 2009; Ohlsson & Sjøvaag, 2018).

Strong incumbent positions have enabled established media companies to assume dominant positions in digital markets (Sjøvaag, Stavelin, Karlsson, & Kammer, 2018). Early digitalization of communication infrastructures, coupled with high media use patterns and comparatively high revenues in the news industries, provided market leaders with resources to innovate (Ottosen & Krumsvik, 2012; Slaatta, 2015), enabling Scandinavian media to maintain their agenda-setting positions (Allern & Pollack, 2017) in the face of growing influence from social media, streaming services and global content aggregators. However, the welfare state model is not without its challenges. Public service broadcasting is under attack from private media operators across the region (Benson, Powers, & Neff, 2017; Sjøvaag, Pedersen, & Owren, 2018), circulation and revenue are declining in the newspaper industry and advertising has moved to global actors such as Facebook and Google. Although policy makers continue to support intervention to protect the mixed system, largely mobilized by perceived threats from globalization, digitalization and personalization, the Nordic systems appear increasingly vulnerable. Movements towards more economic logic and more segmented markets are indications that these countries may be approaching the liberal and polarized pluralistic systems, raising questions about the future of the democratic corporatist model.

Market structure

When Hallin and Mancini outline the newspaper structures of their media system models, they primarily refer to newspaper sales, readership/reach and news consumption figures. For the Scandinavian countries, relevant variables explaining the market structures of journalism extend beyond these basic features to also include the character of their local newspaper structures, media ownership characteristics, digitalization features and revenues.

Brief history

The history of the press in Scandinavia is largely characterized by its social and political history. But understanding the press structures of Denmark, Norway and Sweden also requires an appreciation of how the countries' geographical, topographic and demographic structures have shaped their media landscapes differently. Denmark is small and flat, making communication infrastructures less demanding than in mountainous Norway, where populations are more dispersed; the north of Sweden is mainly forest, centralizing populations in the south.

Norway was under Danish rule from 1537 to 1814 and under Swedish rule from 1814 to 1905. As center-periphery dimensions have been important in the development of political cultures in the region, subjugation also had an effect on media development. While the first printers appeared in Denmark in the 1500s, Norway's first printing press only arrived in 1650, rather late by European standards (Bastiansen, 2014). As such, Norway's press development was affected by the lack of a national capital and organized state bureaucracy (Hovden, 2012). The first Swedish newspaper, *Ordinari Post Tijdender*, was launched in 1654, and the first Danish newspaper, *Extraordinaire Relationes*, launched in 1672, the first Norwegian newspaper, *Norske Intelligenz-Seddler*, did not appear until 1763.

Industrialization and urbanization, however, contributed to the communication infrastructure in all three countries, where telegraphic monopolies were established in the 1850s. Public debates about common suffrage and systems of democratic rule in the late 1800s led to the establishment of political parties, which quickly spurred a mass newspaper market, facilitated by high literacy rates and strong social cleavages (Slaatta, 2015, p. 125). Political struggles in the early 1900s led to the development of the party press system in all three countries, characterized by the presence of multiple, competing newspapers in most cities – usually four papers representing the liberal, conservative, labor and agrarian party interests (Bastiansen, 2014). The party presses began to dissolve in the 1960s, particularly reflecting the introduction of neutral public service broadcasting, and finally ended by the late 1980s or early 1990s. The introduction of welfare state policies in the aftermath of World War II also introduced press subsidies and universal infrastructure policies (Slaatta, 2015). Systems of market intervention have thus contributed a minimum of stability and foresight as the news media faced globalization and digitalization in the 1980s and 1990s. Because Scandinavian newspapers have been locally anchored and associated with organized groups, and because high income levels have sustained both media use patterns and moved users comparatively quickly to digital platforms (Slaatta, 2015), Scandinavian journalism is generally less disrupted than in other countries.

The newspaper structure

Scandinavia has a fully digitalized, decentralized and diversified newspaper structure (Allern & Ørsten, 2011; Høst, 2018). The so-called "omnibus press" has been characteristic of the Scandinavian newspaper markets in the 20th century (Hjarvard & Kammer, 2015). Historically, the Scandinavian newspaper markets have been dominated by five types of newspapers:

(1) Subscription (evening) newspapers, usually liberal or conservative in orientation, corporately owned, and published in large cities with a strong position in regional advertising and audience markets.
(2) Boulevard tabloids or "popular papers" with national publication reach and single-copy morning sales – usually high-revenue papers that were quick to innovate during the digital transformation, leaving them in a leading position online.
(3) Opinion or specialist newspapers that survived the dissolution of the party press system, usually political, religious or sectional in orientation, including the specialized financial press that emerged in the 1980s and 1990s.
(4) Local newspapers with low circulation and low publication frequencies, catering to limited populations usually defined by local municipal political structures.
(5) Free newspapers, emerging in Denmark and Sweden in the late 1990s and early 2000s, segmenting the market by addressing low-income, low-education readers (Schultz, 2007; Wadbring, 2007).

The circulation for print media has decreased since the 1990s. Single-copy-sales tabloids have on average lost half their circulation since 2000. As for revenue, the printed paper is still more valuable than the online version for most newspapers (Krumsvik, 2014). Local, niche and regional papers have retained their market positions even if circulation decline is felt also here. Niche newspapers are doing better circulation-wise than omnibus publications, some even gaining subscriptions. There are few pure players or digital natives in the Scandinavian markets. This is primarily due to the strong position of incumbent players and established subsidy schemes. Most successful online ventures and new media innovation initiatives are anchored in established newspapers and in public service broadcasting (Allern & Pollack, 2017; Barland, 2013); these outlets hold dominant positions in the markets. Although revenue and circulation are dropping, newspapers also find themselves in strategic, incumbent positions from which to assume central roles in the digital news media ecology. Hence, while the large mass-market actors from the analog era are facing stronger competition and larger circulation losses, their corporate organization and resources have allowed them to assume central positions in the digital news infrastructure (Sjøvaag et al., 2018).

As audiences are moving online for their daily news consumption, total daily newspaper readership is declining. Whereas around 80 percent used to read newspapers daily in the 1990s, this figure has dropped to about 40–50 percent. There are now more digital than print readers (NOU, 2017:7). Newspaper numbers are nevertheless holding more or less steady. Norway had 227 newspapers in 2017, compared to 228 newspapers in 2000; Sweden went from 163 newspapers in 2000 to 164 newspapers in 2017, and Denmark retained its 32 newspapers in the same period (Harrie, 2018). Denmark has, however, seen a more rapid decrease in newspaper titles than the other two countries (Allern & Ørsten, 2011). Audience reach for public service broadcasting news also remains above 50 percent, with weekly use at 66 percent in Denmark, 61 percent in Norway and 57 percent in Sweden (Newman, Fletcher, Kalogeropoulos, Levy, & Nielsen, 2017). The high circulation figures for print newspapers in Denmark, Norway and Sweden have therefore been seen as a reflection of a healthy public sphere (Engelstad et al., 2017).

Although free newspapers have affected the newspaper markets in Denmark and in Sweden, they failed to take hold in the Norwegian newspaper market. Hyperlocal newspapers are emerging across the region, many of which were launched in the past 20 years. These hyperlocals tend to complement established papers, filling a gap in the market rather than competing directly. These grassroots initiatives typically have low cost advantages, are dedicated to the local community and are sustained by a mixture of subscription, advertising and press support (Nygren et al., 2018; Høst, 2018).

Localism

Scandinavian media systems are characterized by external pluralism (Hjarvard & Kammer, 2015; Slaatta, 2015), meaning the news landscape is sufficiently diverse to attain pluralism in the overall market. The local press is a distinct feature of these diverse systems (Hallin & Mancini, 2004, p. 150). Due to the dispersed political and organizational structure of the region, a local/regional press served as a mediator between political elites and citizens, as opposed to addressing only a small elite, as in polarized pluralist countries. Newspapers in Scandinavia have therefore been characterized as the "social glue" of local communities (Engan, 2016), serving as communicators between different social and political sectors. As these communities developed liberal institutions early, strong ties between political parties, religion, social class and media were established also at the local level, where most newspapers were socially embedded and anchored (Hallin & Mancini, 2004, p. 153). Because most local and regional markets developed into monopolistic, high-circulation markets, with most communities served by only one newspaper, privately owned newspapers have sustained a comparatively strong commercial enterprise in the region (Slaatta, 2015). An omnibus, "for all" press, coupled with local subscription habits, have made newspapers less vulnerable to digital disruption, explained in large part by the local economic and political newspaper structure.

Scandinavia has a combination of national, market-leading newspapers and local publications. Local newspapers have been the backbone of Swedish (Nygren et al., 2018) and Norwegian (Mathisen, 2010, p. 13) media since the 19th century. Norway and Sweden therefore have a more locally oriented press than Denmark (Fletcher & Nielsen, 2017), due primarily to differences in political structure. The regional political level in Denmark was replaced with larger entities in 2007, and the number of municipalities has been gradually reduced in Denmark and Sweden – a process that is underway in Norway. Sweden and Norway also have regional radio and television, provided primarily by the public service broadcasters. Although newspapers in Sweden have become more regional, concentrating in large regional towns with high populations and production industry (Nygren et al., 2018), Norwegian regional newspapers are becoming more local (Sjøvaag, 2015) – equally concentrated in regional centers, but with a narrowing geographic reach.

The local media structure tends to follow political structures. Most local newspapers cover one or more municipalities. Media "shadows" – areas that are not covered by a dedicated newspaper – do appear, but more so in Sweden than in Norway. Media shadows primarily exist in sparsely populated municipalities and metro and suburban areas outside large towns (Høst, 2018; Nygren et al., 2018). Local newspaper markets have, however, been stagnating since the start of the 2000s, and the number of municipalities with their own newspaper is shrinking in Sweden (SOU, 2016:80). Although local newspaper ownership is more diverse than national ownership across the region, all three countries have seen an increase in mergers of local newspapers in recent years (SLKS, 2017; SOU, 2016:80).

Ownership

Scandinavian countries have similar media ownership structures. Newspaper ownership is primarily private, with a mixture of corporate, independent and foundation ownership (Allern & Ørsten, 2011). State ownership of public service broadcasting is another common feature. Ownership is largely national in affiliation and regional in concentration, with some overlap between the countries. The Danish JP/Politikens Hus and the Norwegian Schibsted are among the companies with newspaper ownership interests across Scandinavian borders. Broadcasting companies MTG (Modern Times Group), Bonnier and Egmont also have pan-Scandinavian holdings, reflecting the extent to which television markets are more regionally oriented than newspaper companies.

Media ownership developments in the Scandinavian countries follow the same tendencies as displayed in other systems such as the United States and the United Kingdom. Most newspapers started out either as family-owned enterprises or were owned by local shareholders, political parties, trade unions and other organizations. Growth in advertising revenue during the 1980s and 1990s made newspapers attractive investments. Because family-owned companies needed capital to expand and invest in technology and infrastructure in the 2000s, most welcomed investments, and some companies also went public. Due to these developments, Scandinavia has seen a concentration and centralization of ownership, both in the broadcasting and newspaper markets (Nygren et al., 2018; Ohlsson & Sjøvaag, 2018). These concentration tendencies were largely characterized by partisan press history. Acquisitions since the 1990s have primarily occurred along old party lines. The Norwegian Amedia, for instance, a foundation-owned company since 2016 (owned by Sparebankstiftelsen DNB), was formerly owned by the Norwegian Confederation of Trade Unions (LO Norway) and the Norwegian Labour Party. Most of the 70 or so newspapers in its portfolio are former labor or social democratic titles. Likewise, Schibsted, a formerly family-owned corporation that went public in 1991, primarily owns former liberal and conservative papers.

Media ownership in Scandinavia is therefore characterized as highly concentrated (Høst, 2018; Ohlsson & Sjøvaag, 2018).

There are, however, also a number of independent companies in the region. Ownership concentration is most diverse at the local level: 70 percent of owners in Scandinavian newspapers are at the local level, and independent ownership mostly occurs at the local level (72 percent). This ownership structure reflects the local character of newspaper markets in the Scandinavian countries. Nevertheless, the digital switchover has presented challenges for independent papers, to the extent that a growing number of independent owners have expressed a wish to sell, preferably to a close corporate title or to a corporation. The advantages of chain ownership in the digital era, including infrastructure in production, content and advertising, mean that concentration tendencies in local markets are likely seen as necessary for survival in the digital transformation.

Digitalization

The Scandinavian media markets can be characterized as fully digitalized. Nearly all newspapers have a digital edition, over half have mounted digital paywalls and digital revenues are increasing in newspaper markets. All three countries have prioritized expansion of digital infrastructures, and internet penetration and mobile use is among the highest in the world (Fletcher & Nielsen, 2017), as is audience use of online streaming services such as Netflix, HBO and the regional player Viasat. Newspapers were prompt in establishing online editions, with the first appearing around 1995–1996, and the region was the first in Europe to switch to digital terrestrial television in 2007–2008 (Ohlsson & Sjøvaag, 2018).

Digital business model development has, however, been more successful in large corporations than in smaller ventures. Whereas newspapers used to operate autonomously, parent companies have assumed increasing control over business strategies, taking advantage of economies of scale in digital markets. The most successful innovators in the Scandinavian markets have been the Schibsted-owned papers *VG* in Norway and *Aftonbladet* in Sweden. These newspapers were quick to build online editions (Ottosen & Krumsvik, 2012), assuming leading positions in the online classifieds markets, and were successful in diversifying into paid problem-solving and consumer–supplier connecting services, such as the classifieds advertising services Finn.no and Blocket.se (Barland, 2013). Joint ventures between telecom companies and leading newspaper brands in the late 1990s managed to create strong content portals and aggregators to counter threats from international brands such as Yahoo and AOL (cf. Ottosen & Krumsvik, 2012). Success in national online markets has therefore largely been a result of brand position and agenda-setting incumbency (Sjøvaag et al., 2018). Overall, the digital media landscape in Scandinavia displays path-dependent tendencies rendered primarily by analog-era market positions, high revenues enabling early digitalization of infrastructures and regulatory policies sustaining incumbents.

Revenues

The newspaper business has historically been a high-revenue industry. Revenue balance for subscription papers in Norway in Sweden was traditionally based on two thirds advertising revenue, but for single-copy-sales papers, advertising revenue amounted to one fourth (Barland, 2013; Krumsvik, 2014). Today, advertising revenue for paper editions in Norway still makes up two thirds of advertising revenue (NOU, 2017:7, p. 53). Hence, the bulk of the income still comes from the paper edition. Nevertheless, digital sales are increasing (Harrie, 2018). In Norway, digital sales amounted to 69 percent of total circulation in 2015, the same year that subscription income surpassed advertising income for the first time.

Although newspapers have experienced significant reduction in income since 2010, many companies are still growing in revenue. This growth, such as that of the Norwegian Schibsted and the Swedish Bonnier, primarily comes not from the newspaper side of the business but from other business ventures (SOU, 2016:80). Nevertheless, market shares of advertising are decreasing exponentially, as the advertising industry moves away from the traditional printed press. More than half of digital advertising revenue now goes to global actors (Ohlsson & Facht, 2017), primarily to Google and Facebook, estimated at 75–90 percent globally (SLKS, 2017). The press has reacted to this loss of income by increasing sales prices, lowering distribution costs (pushing postal delivery later in the day or the day after publication), lowering printing costs by closing presses, increasing the cost of papers delivered to the districts and reducing the frequency of publication (Slaatta, 2015). As Høst (2018) and others have noted, corporate demand for 10 percent plus margins on the back of the financial crisis in 2008–2009, and the ensuing industry downturn in 2012, has not helped matters, particularly on the staffing side.

As the market in programmatic advertising assumes larger shares of the market (approaching 50 percent; SLKS, 2017), coupled with the growth of advertising bureaus and emerging industries delivering data analytics services, corporate media companies are moving towards monetizing the digital traces of their customer base. Data analytics is seen as the new gold in the media industries, leading to increased personalization of content to end users. Online subscription is therefore seen as key to securing future income streams (NOU, 2017:7). As a result, about two thirds of Norwegian and Swedish online edition papers (124 of 191 in Norway and 58 of 171 in Sweden) had introduced paywalls by 2015. However, though Scandinavians are more willing to pay for online news than other European audiences, only around a fifth of online news users pay for news (15 percent in Denmark, 26 percent in Norway and 20 percent in Sweden; Newman et al., 2017). Developments in advertising markets therefore primarily hurt smaller, local newspapers, unable to compete on user data or link up to emerging partnerships based within complex production networks (SLKS, 2017).

Political parallelism

Hallin and Mancini's typology focuses the analysis of political parallelism on the connections between media and other organizations, audience partisanship, journalistic role orientations and the level of instrumentalization of the media. For the Scandinavian countries, relevant variables explaining political parallelism in their media systems in the state/market context can be reduced to two distinct features: corporatism and the party press system.

Corporatism

The relationship between the press and the state/political system has, during the welfare state period, largely been characterized by corporatism. Indeed, Scandinavia has been considered to embrace some of the most corporatist liberal democracies in the world. Corporatism in Denmark, Norway and Sweden has a long history, emerging in the late 1800s and early 1900s (Blom-Hansen, 2000). Corporatism entails organized bargaining, where stakeholders are invited to the table during policy formation processes. Most political processes are therefore consensus-oriented, where parliamentary debate and voting comes at the end of a long process of negotiations involving interested parties at the committee level (Rokkan, 1967). To that end, Scandinavian societies are highly organized. Vocational, political, economic and other interests are formally associated, and most citizens hold multiple memberships in unions, leagues and associations. Representation is key to this system, as process participation is elementary to political decision-making.

However, as Ørsten, Willig, and Pedersen (2017, p. 6) have observed, Scandinavian countries are becoming more fragmented and pluralistic, making classic corporate negotiations slower and more complicated. The decline of corporatism in Scandinavia has been an ongoing process since the 1980s, due primarily to a weakening of unions and stronger parliamentary opposition. Changes in the political structures have also had their effects, including increased localism, municipality reductions and membership in the European Union (for Denmark and Sweden) or the European Economic Area (for Norway). As unions, firms and interest groups lose their seats at the table, they seek influence through other means, primarily through public relations and lobbying. The news media, as such, become increasingly important for political influence (Allern, 2011; Ørsten et al., 2017). The public relations sector, for example, has experienced especially strong growth alongside increasing professionalism since the 1980s.

The corporate nature of Scandinavian consensus politics nevertheless means that media organizations and business have ample access to policy makers. With increasing drops in circulation and advertising income, private actors in the newspaper industries have involved themselves more actively in policy processes (SOU, 2016:80), arguing for more interventionist and protectionist policies in the face of growing global competition (NOU, 2017:7). In parallel with commercial operators lobbying for increased state support and protection, industries are also expressing concern that current regulation is too old-fashioned to allow companies to adjust to new market realities. In particular, competition rules that prevent mergers to avoid concentration in national markets are said to prevent national companies from competing with global giants (SLKS, 2017).

As Scandinavian corporatism has allowed private media companies ample access to policy processes over the years, policy has moved increasingly in the direction of trade policy frameworks over cultural or welfare policy (Sjøvaag & Krumsvik, 2018), a process seen in many other European countries (Freedman, 2005). To that end, economic arguments have become increasingly prominent in discussions about state intervention to prevent market failures. At the same time, Kammer (2016) observes that news organizations are growing increasingly wary that state support systems should be seen as business support rather than welfare policy, not least because this could exacerbate the risk of perceiving media subsidies as a challenge to editorial independence.

The party press

During the corporate era up until the 1980s, Scandinavian newspapers were still locked in a party press system. Hence, newspapers served as "representatives" of different political interests, classes and social groups, working as channels for organized interests (Skogerbø, 1997). Denmark has been found to exhibit stronger political parallelism traits than Sweden or Norway (Brüggemann et al., 2014), but elements of political parallelism still exist in the Scandinavian press at large, visible in ownership structures

(Ohlsson, 2013) and in journalistic opinion genres (Hjarvard & Kammer, 2015, p. 117).

The Scandinavian party press system grew out of polarizing political debates in the early 1900s and consolidated its position between 1920 and 1940. These interwar years were the "golden age" of the party press in Europe, driven by sharp ideological divides (Hardy, 2008). This was an era of economic crisis, social difference, strikes and unrest. Newspapers became channels for political power struggles, and the structure permeated society, from the national to the local level. Party press papers were positioned along the left–right political axis (Schultz, 2007), augmented by the Russian revolution in 1917, which saw an increase in radical, communist and social democratic papers. By pandering to party politics and attacking the opposition, Bastiansen (2014) observes, party press papers increased conflicts in society through their polemic, propagandistic content. Parties often believed in the relationship between the size of their press and election results, to the extent that starting a newspaper in a district could improve results in the next election. Although Hovden (2012) claims that the party press era gave newspapers time to develop a social mission insulated from the logic of the market, Bastiansen (2014) notes that party press papers also exerted economic influence through advertising, being "much more commercially oriented than most have believed" (p. 49).

Although Scandinavian media markets have a history of party press affiliation, the commercial growth of the newspaper industries and the rise of journalistic professionalism severed ties between newspapers and political parties in the period between 1970 and 1990. The decline of the party press has been largely attributed to the introduction of public service journalism in the 1960s. Other reasons include revenue growth in the advertising industry and the search for increased readership, the rise in professionalism through journalism education (Allern & Ørsten, 2011), ownership consolidation and the emergence of publicist and commercial ideologies. The "neutral" press is still the dominant ideal in Scandinavian journalistic cultures, but economic realities are pushing "omnibus" newspapers towards more predictable audience bases, both in the niche and political market segments (Hjarvard, 2007; Schultz, 2007).

Hence, there is a slight increase in political polarization of the press, particularly in the online realm, where "digitally native" publications assume more pronounced ideological editorial positions, typically on the left and right of the political spectrum (SOU, 2016:80). Although there are relatively few digitally native publications entering the news industries in Scandinavia, some of these newly formed news outlets have close ties with organized society; for example, with think tanks and political parties. Hence, though we are not seeing a return to the party press by any means, organizational, ideological and political party ties between media and the political/civil society are growing, not least because these are proving to hold sustainable audience segments. As audiences seem to appreciate a more segmented press, to the extent that opinion or niche papers are also doing better circulation-wise than omnibus papers and new online-only ventures seem to position themselves along a political or interest group perspective, there are signs that polarization in the Scandinavian media landscapes is growing, enhanced by market segmentation processes driven by political parallelism contexts.

Journalistic professionalism

Self-regulation is seen as the main safeguard for freedom of expression (Svensson & Edström, 2016), and protection of the press has a long history. Sweden's Parliament adopted the Freedom of the Press Act in 1766. In Norway, laws protecting press freedom were introduced in the constitution of 1814; the Danish constitution did the same in 1848 (Hardy, 2008). The Swedish constitution even embeds the press in the constitutional separation of state powers. Here, the protection of media expression is stronger than the protection of individual speech (Svensson & Edström, 2016). A formal separation between owners and editors, as well as laws protecting editorial freedom, insulates editors from undue involvement in content decisions. A strong tradition of rational-legal authority has therefore "provided a safeguard against direct political influence on news media, allowing public intervention to go hand-in-hand with an 'arm's length principle' of no-interference in editorial matters" (Hjarvard & Kammer, 2015, p. 117). To that end, professionalism is embedded into the framework of media regulation, with laws protecting publicist industries.

The decline of the party press and the rise of journalistic professionalism are more or less parallel developments in Scandinavia. The expansion of markets as well as growth in revenue also helped journalism professionalize, as the increase in salaries, differentiation in content and segmentation in audiences contributed to create hierarchies in the journalistic profession (Hovden, 2012). Described as high in professionalism (Hallin & Mancini, 2004), Scandinavian journalists are generally educated through journalism schools, and most are organized through national unions. The profession is fully self-regulated, with codes of ethics administered by either a committee system or by an institutionalized ombudsman (Svensson & Edström, 2016). Journalists working in state-owned public service broadcasting are as insulated from ownership involvement as journalists working for private media through the arm's-length principle (Larsen, 2016). The market/state nexus has therefore been conducive to the development of journalism's independence in the region.

The role of the state

Media policy

Scandinavian media systems are characterized by their cultural policy framework, grounded in democratic ideals, open debate and freedom of speech. This policy framework, moreover, emphasizes continuance and stability (Hjarvard & Kammer, 2015; Syvertsen et al., 2014). As such, public funding for culture is embedded in the welfare state ethos of universality of services, and as in other small nation states, protection of national culture and language is seen as important, motivated to ensure an inclusive and diverse public sphere (Bondebjerg, 2016). Public service broadcasting is a significant contribution in this regard, seen as fundamental to the framework of universality and democratic infrastructure in media systems with high levels of state intervention in the media (Kammer, 2016). As Scandinavian markets are too small to sustain cultural and political diversity on a purely commercial basis, market failure rationales are firmly embedded in media law and regulations (Hjarvard & Kammer, 2015). Scandinavian media regulation is first and foremost infrastructure regulation to ensure that external pluralism can be attained at a media systems level, mobilizing scarcity provision, voice, content and exposure diversity aims and ensuring cultural plurality and common arenas for public debate through public service broadcasting.

Liberalization and deregulation have had an effect on media policies in the Scandinavian region since the 1980s, as they have in other countries. Regulators are finding it increasingly difficult to regulate media sectors according to welfare state ideals, not least because convergence makes previously sector-determined regulation obsolete. To solve this sectoral problem, competition frameworks are often introduced as rationales for regulation in place of cultural frameworks. To this end, says Kammer (2016, p. 149), the logic and measures by which Nordic welfare states subsidize media have shifted over recent years. This difficulty is complicated not least by strict E.U. rules on state aid. Nordic states argue that media subsidies are cultural policies, not trade policies (Kammer, 2016), thus emphasizing state support as welfare subsidies rather than industry subsidies. Once policy rationales move more towards business policies, however, the regulatory distance between E.U. law and Scandinavian law becomes blurred, challenging the media welfare state system that state subsidies are built on.

A primary aim of Scandinavian media policy has been to uphold the mixed system of commercially viable journalistic media alongside strong, universal access public service broadcasting. In recent years, as commercial media continue to lose advertising revenue, this mixed system has become increasingly challenged, particularly in regard to public funding levels for public service broadcasting. As policy is largely reactive (Lund, 2016), regulators have struggled to adjust the policy framework to account for the effect of the internet on the two-sided market – the fragmentation of audiences and loss of advertising income to Facebook and Google. The latest installments of policy recommendations in Scandinavia (SOU, 2016:80; NOU, 2017:7; SLKS, 2017), however, address these issues head-on.

As demonstrated by these policy documents, there is still broad bipartisan support in the Scandinavian countries for the mixed media system model with strong public service broadcasting and a viable commercial media sector (Regjeringen, 2017). Policy adjustments are primarily motivated by this balance. As a result, Scandinavian media policies are moving towards stronger intervention, particularly through financial support to commercial players (Ohlsson & Sjøvaag, 2018). These policy shifts are motivated not only by the loss of advertising revenue in the traditional press but also by concerns over increased polarization and misinformation in new media landscapes, audience fragmentation and social media disruption (SOU, 2016:80). Mobilizing all these concerns is the globalization of the media market, which entails a loss of national power over keystones in the Scandinavian media model – including the future of the press support, public service broadcasting and the presence of local media (SLKS, 2017). Media markets are no longer national markets, nor are they segmented along traditional technological boundaries. Facebook, Google, Netflix and Apple are assuming dominant positions in media users' everyday lives. The loss of value chain control – the infrastructure through which Scandinavian media communicate information to citizens – is therefore seen as precarious to Scandinavian democracy, controlled by global, commercial actors (NOU, 2017:7).

Public service broadcasting

Public service broadcasting has held a strong position in Scandinavia, enjoying high public trust, bipartisan support and high market shares (Larsen, 2016). The state broadcasters, Denmark's Radio (DR), the Norwegian Broadcasting Corporation (NRK) and Swedish public service broadcasting – consisting of Sveriges Television (SVT), Sveriges Radio (SR) and Utbildningsradion (UR) – were all established in the interwar years as radio broadcasting monopolies assuming control over scarce airwave resources. Scandinavian public broadcasters were built on the Rethian BBC model, where institutional tasks were to educate, inform and entertain the public, and follow the professional model of broadcasting, run by professionals and isolated from political control. The editorial freedom of the Scandinavian public service broadcasters (PSBs) has been partly secured by their funding system, through a direct license fee (determined by Parliament) paid through television or radio ownership. The license fee makes up 92–98 percent of PSB funding in Scandinavia, a funding system that has come under pressure in all three countries. Whereas the revenue collected from the license fee has been collected by the broadcasters themselves, all three countries are now moving towards a taxation scheme. A likely switch to taxation funding has been met with fears that this would lessen the arm's-length distance between politics and the broadcaster. Budget allocation could be more vulnerable to bargaining and budget debates, making PSBs more vulnerable to political decisions.

Competition in the form of commercial operators was introduced in all three countries in the late 1980s and early 1990s. Each was established with licensing provisions in exchange for the valuable asset that access to all homes meant in the analog-era advertising market, the Danish TV 2 was launched in 1988, while Norway's TV 2 and Sweden's TV4 were established in 1992. All three broadcasters were licensed and legitimated based on pluralist arguments (Larsen, 2016). To that end, the role of the commercial PSBs was to provide an alternative to the state broadcaster, providing both diversity to audiences and healthy competition to the established PSBs. Although the commercial PSBs in Scandinavia have been successful in both the audience and advertising markets (Ohlsson & Sjøvaag, 2018), the state-owned public service broadcasters managed to sustain their strong positions despite this new competition.

Although PSBs have experienced drops in viewership in recent years, the state-funded broadcasters remain strong, particularly in the radio markets (with 70–80 percent daily reach). The influx of streaming services, however, entails significant changes to audiences' viewing habits. Netflix now reaches a third of all audiences in Denmark (SLKS, 2017), Norway (NOU, 2017:7) and Sweden (SOU, 2016:80), and regional players Viaplay and HBO Nordic also assume large shares. Along with new tax-based PSB funding schemes, regulators are discussing ways to strengthen the arm's-length principle to preserve the independence and sustainability of public service broadcasting in the Scandinavian countries (KUM, 2018; SOU, 2017:79; White Paper 15, 2016–2017). Governments are also moving to support commercial public service broadcasting. In Denmark, the license fee is already partly funding the commercial PSB TV 2. In Norway, support to daily news production is included in the latest license agreement between the commercial PSB TV 2 and the state.

Calls for restrictions on PSB online news provisions are nevertheless gaining strength across the region, as commercial newspaper companies lobby governments to decrease public spending on what they claim are market-dominant players hindering their ability to generate income from online journalism. This trend is evidence not only of the precarious financial position of commercial newspaper companies but also of the extent to which media sectors merging into one online platform presents regulatory problems. This conflict signals a potential shift in thinking about media subsidies (Kammer, 2016), which are already visible in Denmark, where the government has signaled a reduction in DR's funding and remit to ensure the survival of commercial news media. Hence, as the advertising market can no longer support commercial news, states step in to improve the conditions of private operators in these mixed media systems, primarily by downsizing welfare institutions in the form of public service broadcasting, making way for business regulation over cultural policy regulation of journalistic industries.

Press support

The Scandinavian countries experienced an increase in newspaper closures after World War II, particularly in Denmark and Sweden. Systems of press support were largely introduced to stop this process by way of subsidizing economically weak papers (Allern & Ørsten, 2011). As this system was introduced during the party press period, high political parallelism in the political bargaining meant the press was deeply involved in designing the system (Skogerbø, 1997). Whoever was in power at the time also had a profound effect on who received press support, and press support schemes therefore came to reflect political power structures (Kammer, 2016, p. 144). Initially, press support was justified as a means to sustain competition between party press newspapers (Skogerbø, 1997), specifically to sustain number-two papers (Nygren et al., 2018) in markets affected by the advertising spiral (cf. Allern, 1996; Furhoff, 1967).

There are, however, differences in how the support is administered. In Sweden and Norway, press support is calculated by the number of subscribers, in Denmark, by the number of "journalistic full-time equivalents" employed (see Hjarvard & Kammer, 2015, p. 121). In Sweden, newspapers with more than 1,500 subscribers and at least a weekly edition can get support (Nygren et al., 2018). In Norway, circulation of more than 1,000 and one edition per week is enough to get support (Høst, 2018). In Denmark, anyone doing journalism can get support (Hjarvard & Kammer, 2015). Press support in Norway and Sweden consists of operational subsidies and distribution subsidies (Svensson & Edström, 2016). In Denmark, direct press support accounts for only a small portion of the subsidies, which is mostly constituted by VAT exemption and reduced postal rates (Allern & Ørsten, 2011). Platform-neutral support was introduced in Denmark and Norway in 2014. With zero VAT introduced in 2016, newspapers no longer had to pay VAT on digital products, which has meant an increase in digital income. Obstacles to digital innovations were also removed by this measure (Høst, 2018). Overall, direct press support contributes very little to the aggregate profit of the industry – only 2 percent in Norway (Slaatta, 2015). Indirect support in the form of VAT exemption is overall a much more substantial subsidy (Hjarvard & Kammer, 2015).

The press support systems in Denmark, Norway and Sweden share common justifications. In all three countries, the support scheme is and has been surrounded with political controversy (Kammer, 2016; Slaatta, 2015). As such, although external pluralism has always been the goal, the rationalization for this aim has shifted over the years (Sjøvaag & Pedersen, 2018a). Though initially intended to sustain competition in the political press, the publicist function is now the primary rationale used by news companies to argue for subsidies. As Hjarvard and Kammer (2015, p. 120) observe, whereas press support was rendered to newspapers as private industries with particular business conditions, digitalization has made these privileges harder to justify, to the extent that Danish press support is now more tied to the public value of the content rather than the particularities of the business. Skogerbø (1997, p. 115) therefore observes the threat that pragmatic changes entail for justifying press support as media structures evolve. The press support has nevertheless undoubtedly shaped the Scandinavian newspaper landscape. For one thing, the number of small, low-frequency newspapers in Sweden and Norway has grown as subsidies began to be targeted to this newspaper type (Høst, 2018; Nygren et al., 2018). The press support therefore represents concrete evidence of the impact that political aims and state measures can have on journalism structures.

Disruption

Most media systems research, while predominantly normative, is intent on explaining how various exogenous forces – such as commercialism, digitalization, homogenization and globalization – affect media systems differently. How journalism is able to withstand, face or use these challenges to their benefit depends on how these professional systems are conditioned by the economic and political foundations from which they have developed. Nielsen (2016) provides an example of such an approach, when discussing the levels of fruition to which three crises of Western journalism – an economic crisis, a professional crisis and a crisis in confidence in journalism – have reached in Hallin and Mancini's three media systems. Here, Nielsen notes that the economic and professional crises are not yet fulfilled in democratic corporatist media systems, but a confidence crisis – a crisis with a long history nonetheless – prevails.

The robustness of journalistic systems is hence thought to be stronger in systems where professionalism is high, whereas market and state-driven systems are more vulnerable to economic and political pressures. To that end, democratic corporatist media systems, and in particular media welfare systems, should be better suited to face disruptions than liberal or polarized pluralist systems. Protection from the market by the state could be seen as a preventative system characteristic of the Scandinavian countries in this regard. As Hjarvard and Kammer (2015) observe, "Whereas many of the technological and economic 'logics' of new media are of a global nature, the historical dependencies of media systems are predominantly national and, in some cases, regional and local" (p. 116). This is why media systems' contexts matter for our understanding of the digital disruption and for journalism's position between the state and the market.

4 Too close to the state

Private media ownership is central to journalism maintaining its appropriate distance to the state. Democracy is based on this – freedom of expression and private ownership is necessary to maintaining the social contract. However, in order to attract serious investors, the journalistic sector needs to be financially rewarding. Fear of market failure has inspired states to support media sectors financially, either indirectly through press support or infrastructure or directly through public service broadcasting. As privately owned journalistic industries experience decreasing income, attacks have been launched against public broadcasters in several markets, with accusations of unfair competition. News industries, particularly number-two news outlets experiencing the effects of the advertising spiral, are also lobbying for increased state support, moving more media outlets into financial dependency on the state. This decreases the boundaries between the state and the media, but distances between the political sphere and the journalistic sphere are also lessening. Both U.S. and European markets have become more polarized in recent years, as news media differentiate to secure an identifiable, stable audience base. Journalism's problem is, therefore, also a problem for state systems that aim for media diversity through the arm's-length regulatory principle. In the social contract, democracy relies on independent editorial platforms to safeguard debate, oversight and freedom of information. As distance to the state is a fluid measure, journalistic professionalism remains important as a proxy for independence. This warrants a discussion of the benefits and disadvantages of state support to media in a time of disruption.

The journalism/state relationship in Scandinavia can be roughly characterized by four features. The first is the particular brand of political parallelism that segments the press into ideological or class-oriented audience groups. In Scandinavia, this has moved from strong in the mid- and post-war era to weak in the decades moving up to the millennium and towards moderate in the internet era. Although the omnibus press is a characteristic feature of Scandinavian media systems, segmentation does exist, primarily explained by the geopolitical and social makeup of these societies. As far as political parallelism explains the close relationship between the state and the media, Scandinavia shares some common features, reflecting in large part the egalitarianism of national cultures and welfare state properties. The related second feature is journalistic professionalism, which is high across these countries. With the dissolving of the party press system, journalistic professionalism emerged as a result of strong moves towards institutional independence. This professionalism signals a distance to the spheres of power. At the same time, professionalism also entails established routines, as well as elite relationships between journalists and the political system, particularly sources. This ties in with the third feature of these media systems: the corporatism that characterizes organized and political life in these countries. Although rational-legal authority has ensured arm's-length distances between the state and, in particular, the organizations and entities supported by the state (such as religious communities, aid organizations and newspapers), corporatization also entails the hierarchical organization of political influence, which means that elite groups have prime access to political processes. The fourth feature that characterizes these media systems is center-periphery cleavages and the strength of local identities, tied in particular to the organization of the political state. Though the countries are quite different in terms of topography and population patterns – populations in Denmark and Sweden being more concentrated than in Norway – their political and economic systems have been characterized by local affiliation. Here, the press has been central to the constitution of local communities, and served as a conduit between political interests as well as instrumental in tying the local level with national power structures.

These press–state features negotiate the distance between journalism and the state in Scandinavian media systems.

Journalism and the state in Scandinavia

The development of the modern press in Scandinavia, as in Europe overall, is characterized by a set of common forces, including the emergence of markets. For these markets to develop, and for trade to take place, merchants needed trustworthy printed and circulated information. The rise in general literacy, helped on by the Protestant Reformation, also contributed to develop information-based markets, the institutions of which emerged from early industrialization processes. Hardy (2008) explains how media system characteristics can be traced to differences within the economy, technology, politics and culture of nation states. Although similarities in how nation states developed can be attributed to the forces of economy and technology, variations between them can be attributed to politics, policy and culture. The market, thus, is seen as a homogenizing force, whereas the state is seen as a differentiating force. The two forces must, however, also be seen in conjunction. Rising forms of capitalism were accompanied by the political liberalism that challenged absolutist systems of rule. Hence, the belief in markets as aggregate places of exchanges in goods, information and ideas emerged together. The history of the European press from the 1600s onwards is therefore often painted as a history of gradual emancipation of the press from the state (see also Curran, 2012). Early state involvement in the press included licensing controls over printing presses, taxation and censorship. Once a mass market evolved for print newspapers, the potential for increased revenues helped newspaper owners and proprietors move away from the close relationship with the state and towards a growing working-class readership base. The commercial incentives that expanded newspaper markets therefore also helped free journalism from state oppression. In this liberal narrative, as Curran (2005) points out, the market is seen as an emancipatory force for good. Here, journalism's independence from the state can only be secured by embedding the media in the free market.

But the free market can also be precarious, largely because of the threat of market failure. Market failure describes the inability of the market to supply the things that people actually need, typically because certain goods and services are not profitable enough to justify the expense of making them, or when people underinvest in these services. People tend to undervalue the externality of services that provide a general benefit to society. It is generally considered good that people are informed. As long as enough people consume news, this ensures a general level of knowledge that benefits social reasoning overall. Once more and more people opt out of paying for these services, however, this externality benefit can be lost. Moreover, once media companies discover that entertainment products are more profitable than hard news, they may divert more resources towards the types of products that ensure return on investment, using fewer resources in the information side of the business. Media subsidies are tools that states can use to compensate for such market failures – providing the types of services that the market is unable to deliver. Achieving welfare state objectives, then, usually implies market intervention. In the media markets, this has typically meant funding of public service broadcasting and newspapers in danger of suffering the effects of the circulation spiral, such as local and niche newspapers. Market failure therefore challenges the notion that states are best kept out of markets.

The mixed media system in Scandinavia implies that there is a balanced coexistence of commercially funded and state-funded media. The state takes care of the unprofitable media enterprises – media catering to minority tastes, small local markets and content aimed at preserving language and culture. This type of state support comes with the arm's-length principle – provisions ensuring that state money does not come with expectations of political support attached. But there are other ways to fund media enterprises where such expectations are present, especially party funding, which has been a staple of Scandinavian media systems during most of the 20th century. As political parties are part of the state system, party support also contributes to drawing newspapers closer to the state. In this context, there is a question about whether the party press system can be said to have delayed the development of the commercial press in Scandinavia. On the one hand, the party press tied newspapers to the political sphere, where party loyalties determined content as well as audiences (Hovden, 2012). On the other, the party press also aligned closely with advertising, exerting economic influence and political power through its advertising departments (Bastiansen, 2014). The politicized party press in Scandinavia was thus deeply embedded in political strife, political processes and struggles over resources.

Although scrutiny of the state arguably reached a hiatus during the party press period, press freedom also involves the right to choose a political affiliation. In fact, political parallelism is a staple of Western media history. The party press actually characterizes most European countries during the interwar years. Not only were the parties emerging as major political forces reflecting social and economic unrest, but the press also developed along with sharp ideological divides in the period. Citizens living in metropolitan areas were usually served by a segmented newspaper market – one newspaper per major party, along the right–left ideological axis. In Denmark, this was referred to as the four-paper system (Schultz, 2007), where each town was served by newspapers answering to the liberal, social democratic, conservative and radical political parties. To some extent, this system entails diversity at the external, media systems level. Newspapers catered to divergent political tastes and identities, ensuring that together, there was a diversity of content and opinion in the marketplace for news. As Hjarvard explains (2007), this kind of political parallelism does not necessarily run counter to the commercial imperative, as political as well as publicist goals can have commercial value in addition to political influence. Neither is it necessarily incongruent with journalistic professionalism, as partisan news organizations often carry more original reporting.

Once the party press dissolved, however, newspapers moved closer to the market – in large part a result of growing economic prosperity and the development of new markets in the leisure and consumer realms. This market proximity was also influenced by the move away from party ownership to corporate and private ownership. As newspapers became corporate, editorial roles became more managerial and less political, and a publicist ideology took over from party ideology. Commercialism, in this sense, can be seen as connected with political neutrality. As commercial values moved into newsrooms, market shares in previously party-segmented markets could only be gained by toning down the focus on politics. The mechanisms of the circulation spiral, which ensure that bigger newspapers attract more readers and advertisers, triggered the closure of many newspapers, particularly in Denmark, and most towns moved towards a one-paper status.

The pull away from the political system is partly influenced by the emergence of broadcasting technology. As European states assumed control over broadcasting spectrum as a public resource, allocating frequencies according to common-good provisions, public service remits that demanded daily news and current affairs also legitimated a more adversarial journalism. The critical oversight that public service journalism should entail ushered in a new era of professionalism, to which newspaper journalism adjusted. Hence, state regulations of media sectors also helped move journalism away from the state and towards a professional ideology working on behalf of citizens and the public interest. However, traces of party-political histories still exist in many newspapers, not only in their ownership affiliations and their charters but also in their reportage. In Norway, this is explicitly expressed in the socialist title *Klassekampen* (Knudsen, Iversen, & Vatnøy, 2018). In Denmark, it is visible in most subscription papers, particularly in their audience base (Hjarvard, 2007). In Sweden, audience segmentation by class is visible in free and subscription paper readership. Free newspapers in Sweden are largely read by people with low income, low education and high unemployment, and subscription papers fare better in the wealthier districts (Wadbring, 2007). To that extent, Sweden has a more stratified newspaper market, and Denmark has a more segmented newspaper market, than Norway. High levels of journalistic professionalism notwithstanding, Scandinavian newspaper markets are not without traits of segmentation and parallelism, despite strong omnibus traditions in the newspaper industries and strong public service broadcasting.

More than anything, the media systems in Denmark, Norway and Sweden are characterized by heavy state involvement. As such, Scandinavian media are already close to the state, not only through direct subsidies but also in the active regulation of media. Strong rational-legal authority, however, also generates a separation of state and journalism. Firmly embedded in policy principles, independence from the state is seen as the foremost criterion for a free media, to which the financial strength of owners is seen to ensure resistance to political pressure (NOU, 1995:3; Holand, 2013). Strong journalistic professionalism, and in particular press ethics, here serves as a guard against state involvement. Although the state may have a certain degree of control over the exchange of privileges for obligations in the media system, self-regulation also renders a certain degree of autonomy in the profession, one that also maintains boundaries between journalism and the market.

In any case, Scandinavian media are in a relationship with the state in some form or another. As recipients of direct production support, over half of the newspapers in the region are dependent on the political leanings of the ruling coalitions at any time. As conservative coalitions often talk about reducing press support and social democratic coalitions tend to support sustaining or even increasing funding to struggling media, this has an effect on how the media reports these issues. Throughout Scandinavian history, political parties have been closely involved in shaping media support systems to ultimately benefit their own political positions. Press support was largely institutionalized to sustain newspapers owned by the ruling parties at the time. Although such extreme parallelism may be a thing of the past, political motivations could always be seen to color these support systems.

To that end, public service broadcasting could be seen as the media organization closest to the state. Public broadcasters are subject to funding over the state budget, determined by Parliament. In this case, the media relies on politicians' favor and the composition of ruling parties. To that end, funding systems in all three countries are shifting towards taxation funding. Ruling parties appoint the boards that oversee the public broadcasters, which also instill a degree of parallelism. The state also issues licenses for commercial public broadcasting in television and radio. Moreover, provisions are dependent on the policies of whoever holds the ministerial office, their priorities and their knowledge of and interest in the media sector. Ownership comes with certain control mechanisms. Where the state owns the media outlet, which is the case with PSBs, the state can instill strong provisions on content, language, staff and budgets. In cases where the state owns the infrastructure, provisions can be put on content balance.

But there are signs of approximations to the state.

Lobbying

Lobbyism is a feature of the political system that erodes the corporatism that organizes political influence in the Nordic media systems. Lobbying requires resources in the form of expert knowledge, networks and access. Both formally and informally, corporate representatives are instrumental in shaping media policy. As traditional corporate processes become slower and more complicated, lobbying presents itself as an alternative means to exert influence. Although the media represent a channel for potential influence over the policy process, media industry stakeholders are themselves lobbying governments for more favorable conditions. As legacy media continue to lose money to substitutes in the advertising markets and audiences to social media, policy lobbying is emerging as an area for sustaining competitive advantage in a time of uncertainty. There has been a string of policy work in recent years with heavy involvement from industry actors. Increased financial support, protection from global players and restrictions on the public service broadcasting remit have been the main subjects of these lobbying efforts.

Here, state support levels are emerging as a yearly battle. As press support is the subject of annual parliamentary budget negotiations, mobilization within the press for sustained support emerges every time there is political movement to cut subsidies. Likewise, debates over the size of the license fee and how PSBs are spending their money are regular occurrences. The fear of Google is endemic among media companies, and there is considerable ambivalence towards Facebook (NOU, 2017:7; SLKS, 2017; SOU, 2016:80). Lobbying efforts are emerging on several fronts at once, fueled by the crisis narrative noticeable in policy documents. Whereas policy in the 1980s and 1990s was colored by caution towards the commercialization of journalism and the growing power of large corporations, policy rhetoric since the millennium has shifted towards industry protection. To a large extent, politicians have bought into the crisis narrative.

Media policy is therefore moving increasingly in the direction of the financial needs of the industry and away from citizenship concerns, continuing its movement away from cultural policy and towards trade policy. Policy is still rooted in role of the media in democracy, but policy initiatives that are being discussed are more in line with financial issues such as barriers on ownership restrictions, press support, taxation of foreign tech giants such as Google and Facebook and employment tax relief for media companies. The main question is no longer what is good for citizens. The main question within this crisis context is what is good for the industry.

Lobbying therefore represents a movement towards the state, as the state becomes more significant in ensuring financial income and incumbency protection. The state presents itself as a safeguard of incumbent media structures. Although regulation has been criticized for being slow-moving and reactive, the industry also finds willing ears within established political structures slow to realize the speed of change within journalistic economies and technologies. This has a reciprocal effect: policy makers are slow to adjust regulation to ensure a healthy media economy and diversity in a globalized, digital media system, and once opportunities for forward-leaning regulatory frameworks are lost, arguments turn reactive rather than proactive. Policy makers therefore also present themselves as more susceptible to arguments on behalf of established systems. Although

Scandinavian countries were early in switching to digital terrestrial television – arguably assuming proactive policy positions within rapidly shifting landscapes – regulation to facilitate the digital shift in the newspaper sector has been slow. Tying press support to the printed edition, for instance, hampered efforts in smaller publications to move towards digital innovation and digital subscription. Instead of incentivizing newspapers to spend their efforts on digitizing their business models, policy ensured that print models remained. This has hurt smaller titles in particular, particularly in the shift towards programmatic advertising, which is heavily reliant on sophisticated data-harnessing algorithms that capitalize on large digital subscription bases.

Media policy frameworks in the Nordic countries have always been intent on protecting and promoting national media for the benefit of media pluralism and democratic debate. Part of this policy has been to buttress strong national players in the face of foreign interests. This is embedded in the nature of small nation states, particularly the need to protect local language and culture. This creates path-dependent policy systems that remain intent on protecting their own system designs. Because relationships between industry players and political players are already established and long-lived, politicians are also more attentive to and attuned to the needs of established players than new ones. The symbiotic relationship between politics and the press has established norms and routines for press–state relations, in which politicians have also invested a lot of time and effort to position themselves. Losing familiar channels of influence and contact with audiences is challenging, not least for political elites, who remain open to the crisis narrative forwarded by incumbent media players.

The precariousness of increased lobbying is that media companies grow ever more reliant on these relationships. Additionally, partnerships are forming among commercial competitors, who largely present a common front, forwarding similar arguments and coordinating policy initiatives towards governments. The problem with this is that policy lobbying requires resources. As a result, the biggest companies often have the loudest voices, leaving smaller local media at a disadvantage. This means that innovative tendencies may go unnoticed, particularly as technology companies are less embedded in the corporate culture, leaving innovation to the established companies. It also creates conflict within the industries themselves as incumbents grow stronger, leaving independently owned and locally anchored media to consider seeking corporate affiliation to latch onto the potential benefits of state protection.

In any case, having too many media dependent on the support of the state is not sustainable for the mixed media model on which Scandinavian media systems are based. Take press support as an example. This is a measure that incentivizes and shapes industry structures. In Norway and Sweden, the lower limit for press support is 1,000 and 1,500 copies sold per week, respectively. This has led to an increase in titles sustainable at this level (Nygren et al., 2018). This may have positive effects for local newspaper structures and their ability to sustain super-local newspapers, but most of these are corporately launched titles rather than independent start-ups. Moreover, large, sustained support to niche papers can spur movement towards niche status within the industries. This is seen for instance in the Norwegian boulevard popular paper *Dagbladet*. Once an omnibus paper, its 80 percent decrease in circulation since 2000 has led the paper to strengthen its cultural profile, from which it could argue niche status, seeking millions in support from the government. If obtained, unless the press support is increased, this would inevitably cut into the funds sustaining other publications that also need this financial basis. As most local newspapers would in fact fold except for the press support they enjoy, shifting the majority of press support towards niche titles would likely affect the local newspaper structure. To the extent that lobbying constitutes a path towards competitive advantage, the strategic resource that lobbyism entails decreases the distance between media and the state.

Attacking public service broadcasting

What is good for the industry, as the industry often portrays it, is to limit the power and dominance of public service broadcasting. Attacks on public broadcasters have been on the industry agenda for over a decade, and it is a trend across Europe (Benson et al., 2017; Nielsen, Fletcher, Sehl, & Levy, 2016). PSBs in Scandinavia share strong bipartisan political support. Private media are, however, arguing that public broadcasters are too big – that they have too many journalistic resources and, in particular, that they are too big online. The argument here is that the open, "free" (although paid for by the public through the licensing fee) online news services that PSBs carry are preventing private commercial media from setting up paywalls and thus securing increased income from online subscriptions. Given the market strength of PSB online news services, the argument goes, commercial media are losing money they might otherwise gain from news-seeking audiences. By curtailing PSBs' online news remits, effectively either establishing login barriers to their news sites or by removing news from these websites altogether, audiences would look for news elsewhere and be willing to pay for it. Commercial media corporations and interest groups are therefore lobbying governments to put limitations on what the public service broadcaster can do online, essentially asking them to stop publishing news on their websites.

PSBs in Scandinavia do have some market advantages that privately owned newspapers do not. Public broadcasters have predictable funding. This means the broadcasters can plan for the long term, largely insulated from sudden cutbacks and consolidations. This creates better working conditions, which attract talent in the industry. PSBs' market pressures are also lower. This means public broadcasters can assume more risk, which creates conditions for innovation and diversity of content. One example of such innovation is NRK's youth-targeted TV series *Skam* (2015–2017), which creators spent a considerable amount of time researching and which ended after three seasons despite massive popularity, even abroad. Its innovative episode structure and social media strategy – short, 5–20-minute snippets of drama released at unpredictable times accompanied by characters' social media presence – was targeted to 15-year-olds, a consumer group not normally on advertisers' radar. As such, the absence of a need for advertising income in itself creates conditions for long-term planning, innovation and risk taking that can often pay off in terms of popularity.

These debates do assume slightly different paths in the three countries, however. Though all three PSBs have pretty wide remits – to ensure a platform for broad and narrow groups, children's programming, quality journalism and current affairs, as well as a forum for public debate, expression and preservation of national language and culture – the breadth of this remit is under constant debate. Often, the question is how public broadcasters should contribute to media diversity: to what extent should they spend their resources on making popular programs, including procuring sports rights? Shouldn't they instead spend their resources on narrow audience groups not catered to by commercial operators? This question goes to the heart of the legitimacy of public service broadcasting as a publicly funded entity. How are citizens' needs best preserved – by catering to marginal interests not otherwise served by commercial media, or by assuming responsibility for ensuring a wide, common platform for expression, experiences, information and debate? Built on the BBC model, the Scandinavian PSBs have traditionally been given both these tasks: to provide a common platform for shared experiences *and* to cater to narrow needs. For PSBs to remain legitimate, however – and, in particular, for the license fee to remain legitimate – the argument has always been that some popular programming is also necessary to attract audiences to a platform where they could also happen upon content they would not otherwise find in the commercial landscape. As such, PSBs have always produced popular formats such as game shows, talk shows, dramas and evening news. And they have aired large sporting events such as the football World Cup and the Olympics. This is because the PSB remit has always been tied to the needs of the public. What is emerging, however, is remit amendments adjusted to the needs of the commercial media industries.

A case in point here is Denmark, where politicians in 2018 made substantial alterations to DR's remit. In the new, bipartisan media agreement, DR was ordered to cut costs by 20 percent between 2019–2023. The new remit also includes a reduction in the content on offer. DR must reduce its linear channels from six to three and its radio channels from eight to five, resulting in a reduction of 375–400 staff, mostly in the sports, entertainment and lifestyle areas. DR's remit still specifies that it should prioritize news, Danish drama, children and young people and regional broadcasts. Although the Danish public broadcaster is to remain a news organization and can publish text-based news online, it is, in the future, to avoid publishing long, thorough news articles on its website. This fear of the competitive effects of PSBs' online, text-based news services are visible also in the Swedish and Norwegian PSB remits. SVT's 2020–2030 remit specifies that the broadcaster should avoid competing with commercial operators online. Instead, SVT should focus on production for audiovisual platforms and strengthen local journalism (SOU, 2018:50). Similarly, the activities of NRK should not appear to diminish the competitive abilities of commercial media. In Norway, the local dimension is also emphasized, through increased cooperation, sharing of resources and overlap avoidance.

While PSBs enjoy high trust and legitimacy among the audience in these countries, as well as high daily reach and bipartisan political support, there are continuous debates about the nature of public service broadcasting in Scandinavian media systems, especially in a time of crisis. To that end, the mantra "the PSB is too big" has settled firmly in the commercial sectors, and private news media corporations argue for a limitation of the remit. These remits constitute political decisions whose source of legitimacy lies with freedom-of-speech principles, plurality norms and diversity aims tied to the media system at large. There is evidence that suggests public service broadcasting has an in-crowding effect on media systems – raising levels of quality in journalism and educating citizens about good media use. That is, it seems the presence of PSBs in media systems makes people consume more news, not less, which ultimately benefits commercial operators (see Nielsen et al., 2016). This is one of the benefits of a mixed media system. The "too big" argument seeks to flip this coin, arguing for a crowding-out effect instead. Here, the idea is that PSBs are taking too much attention away from commercial markets and that, as such, commercial earnings are artificially low.

Public service broadcasting exists in the Scandinavian media systems as an antidote to market failure. The market failure premise concerns the inability of commercial media to give the people what they need. Because commercial media are advertising-based and certain consumer groups are more attractive than others, there is always a risk that these channels will disregard content that serves unprofitable audience groups, such as children and young people and minorities. Media welfare states have instituted public service broadcasting to ensure media landscapes that serve citizens, not only commercial interests. A debate about what kind of content this should entail is necessary to maintain certain boundaries for what a market failure–protecting remit should entail. Although the narrative that PSBs are hurting commercial media's ability to secure digital advertising is gaining strength across the Scandinavian landscape, increased lobbying effects also influence media-political processes that are beginning to assume more industry-wide approaches to media regulation. Hence, public service broadcasting is no longer protected to the same extent. The increasingly detailed provisions that PSBs live under, coupled with more content-specific remits on text formats and earmarked budget allocations, entail greater involvement from lawmakers shortening the arm's-length principle to ensure appropriate media/state distances are upheld.

Arm's-length principle

The arm's-length principle basically explains the principle of editorial autonomy, introduced in the Scandinavian region in the politically unstable mid-war era to ensure that neither state nor market had too much influence over radio content (Lund & Lowe, 2013). Largely applied to the relationship between the state and the PSB, the arm's-length principle goes hand in hand (Hjarvard & Kammer, 2015, p. 177) with rational-legal authority to ensure that public intervention does not mean state interference in editorial matters. To that end, the principle forms a founding basis for cultural policy discourse in Scandinavia (Larsen, 2016). As explained by Moe & Mjøs (2013), "arm's length" entails institutional autonomy. Regulatory powers should here be facilitative rather than executive. Influence is rather set through policy and guidelines, with public bodies operating and implementing policy. The arm's-length principle thus applies to three things in particular: funding, oversight and appointment.

Arm's length in terms of funding is tied to how allocations to PSBs are collected, earmarked and administered through national budgets. In all three countries, the annual license fee is set by Parliament. In Norway and Sweden annually, and in Denmark, a media general license fee (rather than a PSB-specific license fee) is set for four years. In all three countries, fees have been collected by the PSBs. As all three countries shift their funding arrangements from a license fee to a tax fee, the institutional funding arrangements shift, moving the collection and allocation of budgets closer to the political sphere, subject to continued political debate. Moe and Mjøs (ibid) thus note how the size and use of public service funding is tied to political power, making public funding one of the most vulnerable aspects of the arm's-length principle.

In terms of oversight, the arm's-length distance between the state and public broadcasters concerns audit and public scrutiny. In all three countries, regulatory bodies providing oversight of the Scandinavian PSBs are independent of Parliament. All public broadcasters are subject to annual assessment and reporting, including the assessment of their market impact. One important difference here, as Moe and Mjøs note, is that NRK's public service remits are not revised regularly, unlike DR and SVT, whose remits are negotiated with the ruling parties every four years. Although the oversight systems differ somewhat in the three countries, Moe and Mjøs saw signs of increased arm's length in 2013, particularly concerning the autonomy of regulatory bodies. However, regulatory bodies are increasing their oversight activities, particularly concerning the market impact of public broadcasters. Increasing intervention in the form of financial support and ever-more-detailed content provisions also signal increased involvement. As for the appointment and running of the public broadcasters, the Danish and Norwegian broadcasters are owned by the state, to which the Minister of Culture serves as representative of the owner, appointing the board. In Sweden, the public broadcaster is owned by a foundation whose board is appointed by the government, but who in turn appoints the boards of the public broadcasters. To this end, say Moe and Mjøs, the running of the Scandinavian public service broadcasting is formally independent of state involvement.

The arm's-length principle in Scandinavian media systems is primarily tied to the administration of public service broadcasting. Many of these oversight measures are subject to public debate on a regular basis, particularly the license fee and the public service remits. Denmark, as noted, is experiencing a decrease in the distance between the state and DR in recent years, particularly through delimiting remits on content. In essence, all three aspects identified by Moe and Mjøs' investigation of the arm's-length principle in the Nordic countries are dynamic and subject to change. Moreover, political influence to some extent depends on whoever holds the political power, as political parties have different approaches to, in particular, PSB funding models, which have been under revision in recent years. To that end, Powers and colleagues (2017) have noted a weakening distance between public broadcasters and states across Europe. They attribute this, in particular, to changes in financial arrangements, often through shortened funding periods, making public broadcasters more vulnerable to political bargaining within ruling coalitions. Although the arm's-length principle remains "a sacred value in the cultural policy discourse of the Scandinavian countries" (Larsen, 2016, p. 52), maintaining the distance between the state and state-owned media is particularly important as the state is often the subject of critical journalism (Nilssen, 2013). Should distances grow shorter, public oversight on the part of commercial media becomes more important, which is not a bad thing, but one that grows precarious if commercial media lack the funds to engage in costly journalism, particularly in local political structures.

Enlargement of state support

As private media struggle to sustain and grow their revenue in the digital media landscape, state support is emerging as an attractive venue for predictable income. The goal of the state in the Scandinavian media system should be to ensure that an appropriate portion of the journalistic landscape remains privately funded and independent of state support. Whereas state support has been reserved for market failure–protecting measures such as public service broadcasting, niche publications and local newspapers, arguments are shifting towards sustaining legacy, incumbent media. Not only are support measures already structurally geared towards established rather than emerging media, but innovation funds also tend to allocate resources to innovation projects within established media, not to aid start-ups in moving into the digital, publicist landscape. In Norway and Denmark, the commercial public service broadcasters TV 2 (in both countries) both receive direct support. TV 2 in Denmark is partly funded by the license fee. In Norway, TV 2 receives an annual amount in support of daily news and current affairs production.

There is a tendency for private media to move in on direct press support, not only asking questions about the legitimacy of current recipients but also making direct bids themselves. In order to make such bids, newspapers need to satisfy the criteria for press support – either through size, market position or niche orientation (number-two market position is likely to be removed as grounds for support in Norway, per recommendations from the media diversity commission, NOU, 2017:7). As a stable source of additional income, the direct support to newspapers has thus prompted regional news companies in Sweden to launch new, super-local titles sustained at 1,500 copies per week (Nygren et al., 2018). In Norway, the digital strategies of the popular boulevard title *Dagbladet* has put its subscriptions past the 50 percent threshold required to seek press support funding. And the shift in Denmark towards more direct media subsidies in place of indirect support has inspired a need among legacy newspapers to increasingly associate their continued need for state subsidy with a commitment to publicist ideals (Hjarvard & Kammer, 2015). The press support funding could be seen to shift the landscape in a direction of more publicist-oriented, niche and super-local papers. This is not negative in itself, as the support measure is supposed to incentivize these parts of the newspaper structure. But as convergence turns what used to be a variety of support measures into one media support, state subsidies are also prompting actors to instrumentally reshape their profiles according to support rules and regulations.

It is important to note, however, that this media support in itself is not the primary income of private recipients. Subscription, sales and advertising income is more important to the bottom line of these media than state subsidies. But it does entail additional, predictable and reliable income funded by taxpayers to sustain media welfare properties – largely given to incumbent players. Blanket measures such as platform-neutral VAT exemption is, however, more important to the overall economy of media companies. To that end, the industry is not only arguing for increased direct support but also pushing for employment tax exemption. In Norway, this could save media companies 50–60 million euro annually (NOU, 2017:7). This is problematic for a number of reasons, not least because employment tax exemption is already a state support mechanism sustaining businesses in remote regions in the country. For all three countries, moreover, state support to media must comply with competition rules set by the European Union (in Norway's case, administered by EFTA's Surveillance Authority, ESA), which sets limits on the amount of state support that can be given to favor certain private companies over others. This presents legal as well as principle difficulties in sustaining media welfare state systems.

Polarization of the media landscape

As press support also becomes more attractive for neutral newspapers, state support measures to minority and niche media could see publicists moving towards the opinion segment to qualify for support. To the extent that niche paper status releases state support, such incentives could inspire newspapers to attempt to capture issue, opinion or political market segments to secure support, polarizing the news landscape. Although this is not necessarily negative, as it would likely increase the diversity of overall news markets, it does present some problems. We are not returning to the party press, but stable, predictable audience markets are emerging as attractive market segments (Brüggemann et al., 2014), especially along political segments on the right and left. This is particularly visible in the United States, where the media move away from the neutral middle towards positions along the political spectrum (Nechushtai, 2018). Though Denmark,

Norway and Sweden as of yet have relatively few outspokenly right-wing news media or political pure players (examples include *Resett* in Norway, *Dit overblik* in Denmark and *Dagstidningen* in Sweden), these do challenge the principles of press support as a neutral diversity measure. Denying these new publications press support would defy the politically neutral press support, creating a precarious condition where it becomes the prerogative of the state to define what is the "right" kind of journalism and the "right" kind of editorial position. In Norway, both left- and right-leaning publications receive press support (*Klassekampen* on the left and *Minerva* on the right). As creating boundaries for what constitutes too far to the left or right would constitute excessive state involvement, claims of "diversification" support to populist right-leaning media nevertheless challenge the publicist welfare ideals behind Scandinavian media support systems. No matter the outcome of such debates, the emergence of online populist publicists does challenge the value-neutral premises of state subsidies to editorial media – one that constitutes a closer association between journalism and the state.

A further effect of such a movement towards the political segment is that it challenges the omnibus tradition of Scandinavian media landscapes. For the past 30 years, since the end of the party press era, leading Scandinavian newspapers have largely targeted the middle market. National, regional and local papers alike have aimed for large, general reader segments rather than targeting readers along class divides, identities or political interests. This strategy was not only good for securing the largest possible audience and advertising shares; it also created monopolistic local markets and broadcasting duopolies that were able to sustain the major players. Hjarvard (2007) has identified this era in Denmark as the era of the integrated press system (designated between 1945 and 2001), combining popular, political and omnibus newspapers. From 2001 onward, says Hjarvard, a segmented press system better describes the Danish newspaper landscape, where commercial and political newspapers aim to combine commercial and publicist aims. Central to the Scandinavian press system, according to Hjarvard, has been this ideological balance between market forces and public interests, where newspapers have largely aimed at bridging classes and political attitudes.

The omnibus newspapers in Scandinavia have, however, experienced the most volatile changes to their readership base, with sharp, rapid declines in circulation. Although these have also gained leading online positions due to their incumbency and resources, aiming for the middle market is no longer the most lucrative strategy. Online markets can only have one winner for the bulk of the advertising revenue. As niche papers have proved to hold steadier circulation figures and even gains in subscription and sales in recent years, the omnibus news segments could be seen to be shrinking. New entrants to the market, particularly the national markets, are therefore likely to aim for the political segment as a stable option. Along with the erection of paywalls and increased pressures to curtail public service broadcasting online, this decline of the omnibus paper could mean fewer common arenas for public debate and a more dispersed agenda-setting landscape. In a diversity context, this is not necessarily a bad thing, as it results in a multitude of channels that audiences can choose from. However, a trend towards ownership concentration could also consolidate power in the publicist industries, causing too much power to end up in the hands of only a few players.

It is important to note here that there is less polarization in Scandinavian political landscapes than in other regions. There are also signs that these new, "rogue" right-wing publicists are moving towards the institutional middle, seeking membership in professional organizations; for example, in Norway, where the editor of the right-wing website *Document.no*, Hans Rustad, has been accepted as a member of the Association of Norwegian Editors. Moreover, the Norwegian editorial poster has widened its remit to include alternative, political media. Although this could be seen as a challenge to the established journalistic institution, it could also be seen as a process of socialization. As new alternative players are welcomed into the professional fold, this also serves to socialize new players to the institutional standards – widening the boundaries of the journalistic field rather than destabilizing it, to a position where the institution has the power to affect institutional standards.

Legal expansions

Though the diversity of players calling themselves publicist or editorial is increasing, the profession to date seems strong enough to perform the boundary maintenance that is necessary to sustain established definitions of what constitutes "good" and "real" journalism, as opposed to "bad" or "fake" journalism. Scandinavia is not immune to the effects of the "post-truth" era, but professionalism remains strong, as do organized unions, and journalists' rights as well as the arm's-length principle remain protected by law.

Laws are important not only to safeguard journalists' and publicists' rights but also to ensure the proper distance between journalism and the state and the market. Laws do constitute, in a sense, state intervention in the media, but in Scandinavia, most of these laws are based on positive rights – rights to access and protection, for instance. A negative liberty such as freedom of expression is an individual right, but laws pertaining to the media are institutional laws, protecting the roles that journalists perform. Media regulations must, however, balance the need to anchor regulations in democratic and cultural imperatives with industry considerations. Editorial media are not like libraries or universities. Although the press serves a common-good purpose like these other social institutions, journalism must make money on its own, mostly unsubsidized by the state, in a competitive marketplace.

Laws that regulate the media/market relationship are designed to protect journalism from the negative effects of market forces – such as the undue effects of ownership on content. General business laws regulate the composition of boards and worker representation, and labor laws protect workers from exploitation. More specific media laws regulate the amount of advertising that can be placed within or between television programs; press laws regulate the separation between advertising messages and editorial content. Children are also protected by law from harmful media content. As for political advertising, this is more regulated in Norway than in Sweden and Denmark. Although political ads are allowed on Danish and Swedish television, this is still prohibited in Norway, but political parties can advertise on the radio and in cinemas. Political and other types of influence are otherwise administered through professional laws, particularly journalists' codes of ethics, which emphasize the neutrality of reporters as well as the prohibition of taking bribes and gifts in exchange for favorable reporting.

Although there are a number of directives protecting journalistic content from political and market forces and self-regulations to administer professional behavior, the news industries are also regulated by laws governing commerce and industry. Media ownership concentration, for instance, is in Scandinavia not regulated specifically. Instead, it is regulated by competition law. This entails a rather wide separation between the state and the media, as it puts the media on par with other types of enterprises. On the other hand, media industries are also affected by international law, such as E.U. directives (e.g. Directive 89/552/EEC) and U.N. conventions (e.g. the U.N. Convention on the Rights of the Child). Besides child-protection laws stipulating restrictions on harmful content and television directives stipulating common rights to shared cultural experiences (Directive 2010/13/EU), journalistic media are also affected by laws regulating the infrastructures that carry media content, such as telecommunications (for an overview, see EC, 2018), and laws regulating citizens' rights, such as copyright law (COM 2016/0593) and data privacy law (GDPR). Norway, not being an E.U. member like Denmark and Sweden, is also subject to oversight by ESA, which oversees Norway's adherence to E.U. rules mandated through its ECC agreement, which renders access to the European single market. The growing power of large, U.S.-based, globally reaching private technology companies such as Google, Facebook, Apple and Amazon has, moreover, introduced a host of new regulations aimed at protecting European states and their citizens from the harmful effects of concentration in online media markets. Regulating the economic effects of these companies, however – getting them to pay taxes, essentially – is more difficult.

The advertising share of Google and Facebook in Scandinavia is predicted to exceed 70 percent by 2020. States have therefore, either through the E.U. or through the Organization for Economic Cooperation and Development (OECD), begun to discuss opportunities for taxing these companies' operations in Europe. Not only are foreign companies assuming larger and larger shares of these markets, but they are also not contributing to social welfare through taxes that could be used to fund the support mechanisms that sustain marginal media. The problem here is that digital technology generally defies borders, and tax laws are largely tied to physical location (PwC, 2017). Hence, the justification for investigating a "Google tax" is not only the protection of national markets from strong foreign interests but also a question of economic fairness. Reaching agreement on a digital services tax at the European level has been difficult, however, and though Scandinavian politicians are coordinating their efforts (most notably through the Nordic Council of Ministers), uncertainties remain about the effects of such local or regional efforts.

The increasing complexities of power structures within the telecommunication sector, the role of tech giants in national media markets and the implementation of copyright law and data privacy protection signal a shift towards more legal intervention in media-adjacent sectors. Although markets in which income can be sought are becoming increasingly volatile, their legal landscapes are also becoming more complicated, not least because national media regulation in the digital era is losing its jurisdiction over essential infrastructures and resources. Although Scandinavian welfare policies have always strived to ensure that the access of private operators to valuable resources such as the broadcasting and telephone spectrum, which comes with obligations favorable to the general social welfare, states no longer have the power to put the same demands on these new carriers of content – the streaming services that add new content and shift user behavior (e.g. Netflix), the search engines that deliver advertising (e.g. Google) and the social media that deliver news (e.g. Facebook). These operators get the financial benefit of these markets, but states have little power to entice them to do so responsibly, nor to pay taxes. The fact that states are trying, however, to find ways to regulate this new reality entails an enhancement of legal boundaries that moves more and more of the regulatory power to the supranational level.

Policy intervention

To that end, policy intervention in the media sector is increasing. The fear of Google and Facebook is pushing states towards more protectionist policies, the loss of revenue in the commercial sectors introduces more incumbent-protecting support measures and privacy concerns expand legal frameworks to protect citizens' rights in the digital realm. States intervene in the media industries from the structural level to the user level. This is not necessarily negative, but there are plenty of things to be scared of, these days, for media policy makers. Politicians are beginning to wake up to the fact that the internet can also be a precarious environment. Some of these risks carry democratic implications. So-called filter bubbles and echo chambers can separate citizens from the general conversation, drive groups towards extremism and increase polarization, radicalization and hate speech. The increasing use of paywalls in the news industries can deepen information cleavages in society, causing a greater gap between the information rich and the information poor. One newspaper in Sweden, *Dagens Nyheter*, decided to confront this risk during the 2018 Swedish election, choosing to remove login barriers to their content in the time period running up to the election. A relevant connection here is the issue of misinformation, propaganda and fake news – by no means a massive problem in the Nordic region, but there have nevertheless been cases of false information influencing political debates in Scandinavia.

Here, however, there are important differences between the three societies, particularly concerning the polarization within their debating cultures. Denmark, for instance, has been highly affected by the debate surrounding the Muhammed caricatures published by *Jyllands-Posten* in 2005. The publication of images of the prophet spurred violent actions around the globe, followed by ongoing debate over the limits of freedom of speech in relation to religious sensitivity, a debate that spilled over into Norway and Sweden. Likewise, in Norway, the mass murders perpetrated by the terrorist Anders Behring Breivik in 2011 caused debate about the limits of free expression, xenophobia and hate speech. These events and their ensuing debates caused alterations in newspapers' moderation of online debates, primarily through restrictions as to what types of stories were opened for public exchange. As news debates shifted to the Facebook platform, the harsh tone of some of these debates have caused retraction in some audience segments, particularly women, some of whom have experienced threats, misogyny and public shaming on these open forums. Sweden, being the country in Europe with the highest immigration rate, has seen a rise in public hostility to immigration. As established political parties have been reluctant to raise issues of integration, support for the anti-immigration party the Swedish Democrats has increased, causing problems for the political process that stalled coalition formations after the 2018 parliamentary elections, pushing the country into a political crisis. These polarizing tendencies have inspired new publications with outspoken immigration-skeptic editorial positions. Moreover, the online communities where some of these debates take place are largely closed communities.

The polarization of political debate and the fragmentation of audiences have caused shifts in policy concerns towards the end user. In Sweden, the media policy framework (SOU, 2015:94) emphasizes the needs of the media citizen in terms of democracy, information, engagement and responsibility. Likewise, the latest installment of Norwegian media policy recommendations (NOU, 2017:7) emphasizes the need for considering the diversity of content that audiences actually receive and use, not just the diversity of output from media industries. The Danish media agreement (KUM, 2018), in this respect, rests its policy framework on new and emerging user patterns, emphasizing distribution, rather than content, as the crisis facing journalistic industries in Denmark. In all three countries, external factors causing changes in media use patterns are therefore tied to the role of the media in forming the basis for democratic deliberation and participation. It is no longer enough to intervene at the sender side of the spectrum, ensuring that there is a plurality of information and quality journalism in all parts of the country; the reception end also needs to be considered. Whereas audiences' media use cannot be "regulated" as such, regulators are signaling shifts in the direction of the user, emphasizing things like media literacy and even educational programs to teach children to gauge the information environment, spotting the difference between fake news and real news. At the industry end of the scale, concern for the survival of legacy media calls for increased regulation of the activities of the PSBs, and there is more active support of local media.

Scandinavian media policy is becoming more active in the face of all these shifts affecting the news media landscape – not just in the regulation of privacy, free speech and taxation, but also through increasingly detailed attention to the balance of actors in the national and local markets, media use patterns and the culture of democratic debate. Efforts to protect against Google and Facebook entail more protectionist policies to sustain national media, while efforts to strengthen national players in the face of such competition create more intervention. Whereas this entails a continued move towards trade policy and away from cultural policy in how media are viewed as institutions in legislation, the democratic dimension is also strengthened by these approaches. Audiences are not just seen as customers in a market; they are also framed as citizens with needs within a democratic system. Although this may be fully in line with a Nordic welfare perspective on the news media, it does nevertheless entail increased policy intervention in the media, bringing journalism closer to the state.

5 Too close to the market

Journalism operates within a market context where profit is a main driver of success and survival. Nevertheless, the characteristics of markets can also threaten journalistic autonomy, legitimacy and credibility. Unlike other products, journalism needs to sustain a proper distance from market effects on its main content, the news. Although private ownership and profit motives are essential for the democratic role performed by the news industries – securing institutional independence and sufficient distance to the state – markets also constitute threats of failure.

The threat that markets can sometimes fail to provide people with the products and services they need constitutes the insufficient allocation of goods and services in a free market. Market failure can occur for a number of reasons, most of which, in the media sector, are linked to externalities, free riding and monopoly situations. Externalities, in this context, refer to third-party effects. Positive externalities, which journalism potentially enjoys in abundance, mean that individual consumption has a positive effect on others, such as the fact that the heightened awareness of public issues in the public serves society at large. Negative externalities, on the other hand, occur when self-interest keeps valuable products from surviving in the market. Journalism also potentially has a lot of these negative externalities, as companies' economic self-interest can lead markets to produce only what people want. Consumers' self-interest can also lead to negative impacts. Many media products can in principle be consumed without paying for them. Consumers can watch television in someone else's house, borrow their neighbor's newspapers and find news online for free. The free-rider problem can prompt producers to stop producing such products, which hurts society at large. State intervention in markets is usually tied to these effects, ensuring that public goods such as education, roads and national security that benefit all do not suffer market failure effects.

Public goods are characterized by non-rivalrous consumption and non-excludability. This means the consumption of one person does not exclude the consumption of others. Unlike toothpaste or shampoo, one person's consumption of a television program does not prohibit other consumers from enjoying the same product. If too many people fail to pay for valuable products, such as investigative journalism, the incentive to produce more of those products will disappear. Monopoly power, on the other hand, generally tends to set prices too high, hindering competition that may benefit users. Hence, there are many market incentives that can lead media owners to underproduce social value from journalism.

Keeping a good distance from the market thus means journalism should avoid becoming too commercialized. When news media only give the people what they want, such as sports, entertainment and lifestyle features, rather than what they need, such as information on what the government is up to, the social benefits of journalism are lost. The traditional bundled model that was the printed newspaper served to balance the negative effects of externalities: people might buy the newspaper for sports, cartoons, obituaries or crossword puzzles, but they also get doses of valuable political, social and financial information just from flipping through the pages. Market-attractive content such as travel and lifestyle journalism, sports coverage and gossip columns hence serve to subsidize less attractive content, such as journalism covering the courts or Parliament. Because advertisers were more attracted to the type of content that could lead people to consume – holidays, furniture and clothes, for instance – newspapers would profit from producing sections on travel, homes and fashion, more so than they would profit from producing politics sections.

When news is unbundled online, direct access to market-proximate content could lead consumers to skip information with positive externalities, going straight to entertainment. As online advertising was cheap compared to print, the value of readers declined, and market-attractive journalism became less profitable, with decreasing subsidies available for political journalism as a result. As the bundled model crumbles, more forms of market-approximate forms of content emerge, including content marketing. Not least, when profit demands from owners remain high in a market of decreasing returns, expensive journalism suffers, whereas content with market potential is on the rise. Moreover, the search for profitable ventures increases as news organizations struggle to find new income streams to subsidize public-good journalism. More detailed information on the user emerges as a new product that can be sold to advertisers, creating gaps between resource-rich companies able to collect and analyze data on logged-in digital subscribers and resource-poor organizations that are still largely analog, such as local print newspapers, which fall behind. Moreover, click-focused, user-interest and advertising-driven online news strategies move journalism closer to the market, adjusting to new demands from advertisers and lower income streams, threatening the legitimacy of the profession as well as the institution.

This all makes the market realities facing journalism in the digital realm rather precarious. But the market is also a source of strength for journalism. In fact, the market realities of the Scandinavian countries are arguably what have made Scandinavian news markets comparatively strong. Characteristic of these markets are three aspects: private ownership, omnibus news media and journalistic professionalism. The positive effects of these market realities are all tied to the social organization of society, in particular a corporatized civil society, welfare capitalism, economic growth and strong unions.

Private ownership

The development of press systems is essential to Hallin and Mancini's media system models. In Scandinavia, unlike in southern Europe, the press developed as an information channel connecting citizens, through religious, civil, party and other organizations, with political power. Whereas newspapers in other regions served as channels for conversations between the elites, the organization of Scandinavian newspapers helped tie the citizenry to political processes. This was not least due to essential social and geographic cleavages that made local newspapers important to local communities – part of the reason, as Hallin and Mancini (2012) note, why newspaper structures have remained relatively decentralized in the region, and not least, sustained their readerships. The center-periphery divide that has characterized resource and interest conflicts in Scandinavian politics meant that local communities developed liberal institutions early, to secure their interest against centralized power. Because the press tended to be rooted in political and cultural sub-communities, organized groups and their press played a central role in the structuring of political and cultural life, anchoring journalism to local identity as well as political processes. Newspapers were owned either by families or cooperatives with a few large owners – usually municipalities, parties, organizations or unions – and many small local shareholders (Holand, 2013). Private ownership therefore not only served to distance journalism from the state system in this respect, but also associated journalists with local and interest communities.

The emergence and growth of newspaper markets in Scandinavia, as in the rest of western Europe, is not only tied to the development of nation states, democracy and a system of parties and unions; it is also tied to processes of industrialization and the emergence of market institutions. While industrialization developed later in Scandinavia than elsewhere, newspaper growth was stimulated by the rise of capitalism, mass literacy and an emerging merchant class. The shift to industrial production in the late 19th century meant the costs of newspaper operations grew. This shifted ownership towards industry and led to a concentration in ownership, mass-market orientation and the development of salaried, unionized, professional journalism. As the press developed into a large-scale, capital-intensive industry, reliance on advertising also grew (see Hardy, 2008, pp. 33–35). Ownership within this development was largely tied to wealthy business owners that saw political as well as economic benefits in newspaper ownership. These companies often assumed the form of family ownership as control was passed down through generations.

As the party press emerged, this was largely driven, as Ohlsson explains (2013), on the initiative of private owners aligning themselves with political power. And though Denmark and Sweden developed foundation ownership forms to protect newspapers from the demands of profit maximization, foundations also often had political ties. Organized Scandinavian society lost control of the press by the 1970s, from which a professional model of private ownership emerged. Newspapers moved from party, union, religious and community ownership to corporate ownership, the largest of which went public on the stock market. Despite the rise of public ownership, the majority remain in national hands; this also inspires concentration to counter the strength of potential foreign buyers.

Today, the majority of newspapers in Scandinavia are privately owned. Acquisitions are on the rise, particularly in the local newspaper segment, as small local titles struggle to remain profitable in the shift to a digital subscription and advertising model. Many of these local papers actively seek corporate ownership, primarily by approaching their closest large corporation. The advantages of corporate structures are gaining in significance, especially as programmatic advertising is on the rise. Small local newspapers that have been slow to shift their readership towards online subscription are failing to monetize the advertising value of their readership base. Not only do they lack the technical resources to harvest and analyze digital user data, but their independent status also makes it more difficult for them to profit in the market for programmatic advertising. Even local newspaper chains are too small to operate sustainably within this market. In Norway, the southwestern-based newspaper chain Nordsjø Media, with nine titles, was bought by Amedia in 2019. At the same time, Swedish MittMedia, with 38 newspapers, actively sought corporate affiliation, and was bought by Bonnier News and Amedia in 2019. Hence, stronger advantages of corporate ownership emerge, particularly in terms of securing a sufficient digital infrastructure, algorithmic data curation and advertising potential.

The trend towards ownership concentration speaks not only to the rising cost of newspaper ownership and operation. Although the online environment once had low barriers to entry – meaning essentially anyone could launch a news website with little cost (especially costs tied up in printing and distribution) – online publishing now demands more resources. The demands of the technological infrastructure speak to scale advantages more than before, particularly as the need for innovation in digital revenue generation becomes reliant on an increasingly specific skill set set outside the traditional journalistic toolbox. Not only are coders moving into advertising and marketing departments, they are already present in the newsroom – in "robot" journalism streamlining news production in the areas of sports, finance and politics.

The new algorithmic environment is overtaking the business as well as the editorial side of news. This puts new demands on news managers, requiring increasing sophistication to survey the competitive environment. As a result, newspapers see the need for an ever-more-professional media management, leading smaller titles and corporations to seek scale advantages among the large corporations. One effect of all this is a concentration of ownership power across the region. And though the trend of algorithmic curation, production and management certainly frees up the resources needed for thorough, investigative journalism, it also expands news operations' knowledge base needs in the areas of business and management, shifting strategic control towards market-approximate skill sets.

Omnibus news

The egalitarianism of Scandinavian society has meant that news markets have been largely unable to segment across mass/elite divides. Unlike the United Kingdom or Germany, there have not been large enough audience segments in the upper classes to sustain elite newspapers oriented towards the rich and highly educated. Nor has there been a market for outright "tabloid" papers targeting "lower" classes. Although a financial press has developed in these countries, newspapers have primarily aimed for mass markets. These socio-cultural conditions shaped newspapers in the post-party press era into omnibus publications, targeting a general audience. The Norwegian press historian Martin Eide has thus described the boulevard papers in Norway (in particular, *VG* and *Dagbladet*) as schizophrenic (2004) – both popular and serious at the same time. To that end, leading dailies in Scandinavia have followed a mass-market-oriented strategy, aiming to maximize readership with popular content while securing strong agenda-setting functions through investigative political journalism. Although these leading national dailies have secured leading positions online due to their analog status in the market and considerable corporate resources, these titles have also lost the most circulation since the introduction of the internet, up to 80 percent for the Norwegian popular papers. The market losses of these omnibus leaders do not spell the death of omnibus journalism in Scandinavia. However, they do signal a shift towards market segmentation. As fewer of these popular generalists can survive in the market, save as free newspapers (e.g. Hjarvard, 2007), newspapers need to secure predictable audience bases, moving towards stronger editorial identities. Indeed, the most successful newspapers in this shifting landscape have been local and niche publications – titles with clear editorial profiles and publicist identities.

Hjarvard (2007) describes this shift in the Scandinavian newspaper markets as functional differentiation – strategies aimed at ensuring audience segments. According to Hjarvard, the Danish newspaper market has split along a commercial/publicist divide, where commercially oriented papers follow a free model and publicist papers follow a subscription model. Although the homogeneity of Scandinavian society meant newspaper markets largely bridged classes and political attitudes, balancing journalism between market forces and public interest, the volatility of the online economy upsets the omnibus character of journalism in Scandinavia towards a more differentiated system. The omnibus papers were, after all, the drivers of a free news culture online. As their digital presence grew in strength, readers flocked to the online substitute and stopped buying the printed product. The problem of substitution thus hurt the omnibus generalists the most, as they were also in a competitive situation that did not affect local and niche papers to the same extent. Striving for monopoly situations in targeted markets therefore emerges as a strategy for predictable income, shifting the news landscape towards functional differentiation.

Journalistic professionalism

Within the field of political communication, journalistic professionalism is largely thought of as the mechanism that separates journalism from political power (e.g. Hallin, 1994). But professionalism is also a fundamental notion protecting journalism from market forces. Not only does it raise practice from vocation to exclusive expertise; it also comes with a set of boundary-protecting mechanisms – including self-regulation, ethics, public service orientation and socialization norms. Alexander (2016) thus refers to professionalism as the wall that stands between journalism and the business side of news. As Alexander contends, "Business managers devote themselves to trying every which way to commercialize the products of journalism, but crafts persons, not owners and managers, create the news" (2016, pp. 7–8). There is thus an oppositional force embedded in professionalism that serves the legitimacy of the field. As such, professionalism insulates journalists from the effects of the market.

Örnebring (2010), however, has noted an increasing volatility in journalistic labor rights, particularly through de-skilling, differentiating work processes and introducing technology to increase efficiency. To him, these trends are continuations of constant and historical adjustments of journalistic labor to market realities. Technology, in this framework, is an instrument of productivity, efficiency and corporate control. As Örnebring remarks, "The discourse of speed, understood as at heart a capitalist logic of competition and use of technology to increase productivity, has become a wholly naturalized element of journalism and forms a template for how journalists understand new technologies" (p. 66). Journalists are, after all, employed by businesses that need to operate in a market. Hence, in a critical political economy perspective, professionalism has been read as part of the framework that serves to commercialize journalism (Bagdikian, 2004; McChesney, 2003). Here, professional autonomy is rendered to journalists to ensure public legitimacy, which protects the institution from claims of bias, which in turn ensures advertisers of editorial neutrality, expanding newspapers' market potential.

In journalism studies, however, journalistic professionalism is a self-protecting measure that serves as a lever enhancing freedom from the state as well as the market. Indeed, Ryfe (2017) sees it as one of the forces that "pushes" on journalism. In Ryfe's tentpole analogy, journalism is pulled by the external forces of the state and the market, while professionalism pushes back on these external forces as an internal force. In Ryfe's analysis, the market has lost much of its strength in pulling on journalism, causing there to be less for the profession to push against, prompting permeable boundaries and weakening integrity. Such field disintegration is strongest, Ryfe contends (p. 139), where journalism is highly exposed to the market.

Professionalism is, however, often the default setting in maintaining the boundaries of the field – not just towards the market, but also to other activities that threaten journalism's legitimacy. A rise in competing forms of information dissemination, such as amateur reporting, blogging, hacking and propaganda, forces journalism to engage in boundary demarcation – signaling to the outside world the difference between what is journalism and what is not. The arguments forwarded in this regard are often associated with journalists' professional methods. Guidelines for how to spot the difference between real and fake news, for instance, focus on genre traits and practices: who are the sources, and how many of them are there? How many points of view are included in the text? What is the writing style, and to what extent do headlines follow professional norms? Caps lock and exclamation marks are not generally used for effect in journalism. Nor do news organizations let outrageous claims stand unopposed. Likewise, hacking is not journalism. Although WikiLeaks' information campaigns bear some resemblance to journalistic investigation, simply dumping documents in public spaces is not the same as doing journalism. Information needs to be edited, curated and checked.

The claim to professional legitimacy therefore largely lies with the things that journalists do. Moreover, it is embedded in the editorial institution – the framework under which news is produced and disseminated. In this context, journalism as an institution is facing certain challenges with the rise of politically motivated, right-of-the-right online news sites. Scandinavia has seen a slow emergence of some of these sites. Sites such as *Document.no*, *Resett*, *Frihetskamp* and *Rights.no* in Norway, *Dit overblik* in Denmark and *Nya tider*, *Samhällsnytt*, *Fria tider* and *Nyheter i dag* in Sweden are all producers of immigration-skeptic newslike content that drives debate and online traffic. When Helge Lurås, the editor of the Norwegian site *Resett*, applied for membership to the Association of Norwegian Editors, the outright rejection of his membership by the Association spurred debate about the boundaries of the editorial institution. Is it only to be reserved for "neutral" publishers? If politically motivated publishers are OK (such as *Minerva*, the online news site run by the conservative Norwegian think tank Civita, now a recipient of state press support), are some politics less OK than others? In a freedom-of-speech context, where is the line drawn? In the case of Lurås' membership, the Association had three main grounds for rejection (Nored, 2018): repeated breaches of the codes of ethics, incidents of paid sources and encouraging readers to boycott other media.

To that end, the boundaries of journalistic professionalism remain protective in the face of a growing partisan media sphere that only pretends to be truly journalistic. Not only is exclusion here based on established ethical norms, but the outsider himself also acknowledges the borders of professionalism by applying for membership. There will likely be more cases of boundary challenges as the number and reach of partisan media appear. However, though professionalism might be able to withstand such jurisdictional challenges, the question remains: to what extent does the public reached by these sites really care? This is a far greater threat to the journalistic institution – the disassociation from audiences who feel their information and deliberation needs are not met by mainstream media. The stability of these audience groups not only serves a political purpose but also provides income bases for advertising.

Journalism and the market in Scandinavia

Market trends in Scandinavian journalism point to a concentration of ownership and a differentiation of the press structure. These are economically motivated trends brought forth by the realities of the digital economy. Signs of proximity to the market in Scandinavian journalism can therefore be seen both in the press structure and in the editorial room. Because journalism's main sources of income, audiences and advertising, are increasingly powered by surrounding digital and social media industries and money is shifting upwards in the system towards global platforms and players, journalism is losing control over its markets. Advertisers go where audiences go, and as audiences migrate towards social media, advertisers follow. Journalism's relationship with the market is thus affected in large part by forces operating outside the field. As a result, editors and news managers start moving their product in the direction of these markets. The growing power of the market is felt in every part of the structure, from the infrastructure that carries journalistic content – telecommunications as well as social and mobile media – to the technologies that ensure digital income: programmatic advertising, paywalls and content marketing. The market pull on journalism is about both saving money and generating new income. All signs point to these resources shifting upwards, both in terms of infrastructures and geographies, changing the power dynamics of the journalistic industries.

Telecommunications

As the access to audiences and advertising moves up the chain from content producers to content distributors, income streams are affected across the journalistic landscape. In the television sector, content providers – basically television channels – held good cards in their relationships with cable distributors for many years. Their valuable content was what secured cable subscribers, and channels could demand increasing payments from operators by threatening to take their content to another distributor. As cable companies lose their place in the value chain, being surpassed by fast broadband and mobile internet access as well as streaming services delivering content directly to viewers, their position is weakened. As a result, cable operators are joining forces with telecommunications companies – formerly the owners and operators of telephone infrastructures that transitioned successfully into internet service providers. These companies have made efforts to secure content of their own in recent years, bypassing the cable part of the chain, particularly in the valuable sports rights markets. They are also moving towards building their own payment and subscription systems to capitalize on valuable audience data from comprehensive customer registers.

These structural changes in the mobile and telecom markets affect broadcasting markets in terms of content and audiences. Television channels grow weaker as the bidding over sports rights grows fiercer. This is important because sport is arguably the most valuable content in the media industries. Not only does it provide live, attractive content that generates advertising revenue, but it is also the only content that is able to move users easily towards new providers. Sports fans can sustain higher switching costs than other user groups. Their interests and loyalties lie with the team, not the content provider. Thus, securing the rights to a popular sports league can mean potentially hundreds of thousands of new customers – securing valuable subscription revenue and predictable advertising income. At the same time, traditional broadcasting faces competition from streaming services. Netflix now reaches a third of all audiences in Denmark (SLKS, 2017), Norway (NOU, 2017:7) and Sweden (SOU, 2016:80), and regional players Viaplay and HBO Nordic also assume large shares. As a result, broadcasting companies are increasingly seeking partnerships with telecom companies.

A case in point here is the Scandinavian broadcasting market. The Danish, Norwegian and Swedish telecommunication giants are moving in to secure ownership of the largest broadcasters in the region. In Denmark, the privately owned telecom TDC (Tele Danmark Communications) has acquired MTG, a broadcaster that reaches 10 million viewers across the region, and in Sweden, Telia (where the Swedish state owns a 37 percent share) has acquired Bonnier Broadcasting, formerly owned by the Swedish publishing company Bonnier, the largest media company in Scandinavia. When Telia acquired Bonnier Broadcasting, it took control over the commercial channels TV4, CMore and MTV3. In addition, Telia bought TDC Norway (the Norwegian branch of the Danish telecom) and merged with its Norwegian cable distribution company, Get, in 2019. The Danish publishing company Egmont has also moved to consolidate operations in the broadcasting sector. It already owns the Norwegian commercial public service broadcaster TV 2, and it is moving in to secure 40 percent of its Danish counterpart, formerly owned by the Danish state. Broadcasting markets in Scandinavia are not only moving from state to private ownership; ownership itself is also moving up in the system, concentrating power over content and distribution to a few dominating telecommunications companies that were once established and owned by the states.

This follows an international trend marked by telecom companies moving in to secure content. British Telecom in the U.K. and AT&T in the U.S. are both building their content portfolios to secure audiences in the future. Broadcasting is thus moving towards integrated structures where a few major players aim for ownership of distribution, content and customer data, securing complete control with ISP, mobile, cable and content in one chain. Ownership is thus not only concentrating in the newspaper market; consolidation is on the rise across the media landscape. On the one hand, this shifts the power over information markets into the hands of a few key players – a potential cause for concern in terms of access, diversity and oversight. On the other hand, this concentration also strengthens the position of regional players, making them stronger in the face of potential acquisition by foreign conglomerates. The concentration of markets globally thus has a regional effect, where market realities force oversight bodies to accept these mergers, or else the needs of national market protection to safeguard national language and culture may suffer.

Social and mobile media

Social media platforms are one form of global ownership that has well and truly made an impact on national media markets. Even though most, if not all, Scandinavian news media have a social media presence, news organizations are losing ground to Google and Facebook as users seek news online: 87 percent of audiences in Norway and 86 percent of audiences in Sweden now use online media (including social media) as sources of news, but only 36 percent and 39 percent respectively use print media. Danish media make massive use of Facebook as a distribution channel, posting 92 percent of news stories to their Facebook pages (SLKS, 2017). This online information-seeking behavior means news media are forced to target these audiences through free content. At the same time, recent changes to Facebook's algorithm means that news stories from these pages are becoming less prevalent on users' news feeds. In addition, local community information sites are emerging on Facebook, competing with local newspapers for audience attention. Particularly in Sweden, local groups on Facebook play an increasing role (SOU, 2016:80).

The problem with Facebook for news media is that the income model rendered by the social media site is of less value than reaching audiences on the platform. Facebook's Instant Articles initiative has provided little income, and most media houses have left or down-prioritized the platform. This is not least because news outlets lose out on valuable user and traffic data. Building platforms of their own where this data can be harvested and used is a sounder economic strategy. This reality is connected to smartphone use, which is high in the Scandinavian region at over 60 percent (Newman et al., 2017). As mobile use overtakes desktop use, figuring out how to advertise on the handheld platform becomes a priority, not least because media use among younger demographics points to new channels of news consumption such as YouTube, Snapchat and Instagram. News media are trying new ways to reach these younger audiences, who often feel disengaged from established online and mobile news formats.

Developing the technology needed to sustain user engagement on the mobile device therefore becomes imperative for the news industry, as the technology itself places boundaries on the content. The screens of smartphones and other devices are hard to read in sunlight, and sound pollution from video play in public places is changing the way news organizations are designing videos. Heavy use of advertising can slow download time, autoplay is often seen as annoying and advertising takes up much more space on the screen. But mobile also holds large potential for advertising growth, as it reaches people on the go, and is therefore closer to their purchasing contexts (Solvoll, 2017). New markets in social and mobile media therefore affect content priorities, design and production, as media use situations shift towards continuous use.

Programmatic advertising

The massive growth in mobile use means, however, that Facebook and Google are increasingly important, as media as well as advertisers have to reach people where they consume content. Not only is distribution seen by the industry as the key to attain user involvement – such as sharing and linking content on social media (Krumsvik, 2018) – but the rise in search and video advertising means Facebook and Google are driving advertising trends. More and more of this digital advertising is handled by ad agencies linking buyers and sellers. Half of display advertising revenue in Europe in 2018 was traded programmatically (IAB Europe, 2018). Whereas in the analog era, advertising was largely a transaction between newspapers' marketing departments and local retailers, often through personal encounters, digital advertising entails packaging based on target group analyses and strategic planning based on user data. Although such programmatic advertising allows for more targeted consumer strategies, these processes are also less transparent. Advertisers in this context largely lose control over where ads are placed – on what platforms and next to what content. There have already been instances of large brands withdrawing from Google's AdSense after their ads were placed next to hateful content on YouTube. To that end, programmatic advertising can also be gamed, for instance by bots programmed to boost a site's popularity to drive up advertising revenue (Ohlsson & Facht, 2017).

Programmatic advertising relies on data about user behavior. News organizations therefore need to invest in the resources required to handle this transition. Not least, they would be wise to develop data on their own users and not yield valuable resources to advertising agencies. To that end, generating digital subscribers that stay logged into the system is paramount to collect the data and insight needed to generate value for advertisers. This data can consist of web metrics and web analytics, statistics on advertising impressions and advertising performance, content analysis of news stories, subscription data, financial reports and background data on paying as well as non-paying users. This operation can require large resources in the form of data warehouse infrastructures, data scientists and marketing suites. Not least, combining subscriber and advertising information requires coordination of competencies formerly held in separate departments, entailing a certain change in newsroom organization, culture and management. Such an infrastructure can enable automated marketing – the algorithmic triggering of preset tactics for content and advertising based on individuals' behavior on the site. The goal behind this data turn is essentially to drive on-site engagement, increase advertising profits and ultimately turn non-subscribers into subscribers (Kiesow, 2018).

The need for such infrastructure and digital know-how is a major factor shaping news landscapes in Scandinavia. For one thing, this shift is driving ownership concentration in the newspaper sectors. Large organizations have been better at mounting a digital strategy, not least because they have the resources to invest in the right skills and technologies to enable a move towards user data. Centralized data strategies benefit the chain at large, not least because these companies can afford to develop tools in-house? test different options and customize solutions based on different market needs. Smaller, typically local and independently owned newspapers are at a disadvantage in this context. They have not only been slow to convert readers into digital users but also remain stuck in analog advertising markets. As local businesses move to Google for their targeted advertising needs, local papers lose out on valuable income. Moreover, they lose out on valuable data about what is usually a highly loyal, engaged and non-substitutable local audience. As local newspapers in Scandinavia are largely disconnected from the hyperlinked network (Sjøvaag et al., 2018), their non-participation in the digital news ecology means these titles are falling behind in the emerging advertising markets. Many of these small newspapers realize as much and have begun actively seeking buyers with larger organizational structures. Particularly in Norway and Sweden, local newspapers are seeking corporate ownership to avoid falling behind in the programmatic turn, something that leads to a concentration of ownership.

Paywalls

A key to amassing this data resource is logged-in users. News organizations need to know who their readers are and how they behave in order to capitalize on this new industry "gold" – both to drive user engagement and to attract advertising. The Scandinavian newspaper industry was quick to realize this potential and began implementing digital paywalls as early as 2013. First, subscription barriers to access online news content was mainly a strategy aimed at keeping the current print readership, hoping to slow down the decline in subscriptions. Once a significant portion of subscribers had been converted, the strategy turned to reaching new readers. Then, it became about user data, needed to understand what can trigger audiences to subscribe. As these goals shifted, so have audience relations. Digital subscription is no longer just about the number of readers but also about the types of readers and their reader experience.

About half the newspapers in Scandinavia have built digital paywalls. The success of these strategies has attracted the attention of news organizations worldwide. In most of these papers, content performance data is on prominent display in the newsrooms. Journalists in these newsrooms know more about how their articles, videos and podcasts perform among paying and non-paying audiences than ever before. They know what kind of users engage with their content, how much time users spend with the content and where they go next. There has been some concern both in the industry and in academia about the effects of these user metrics on journalism. When story performance is monitored closely, editors have more direct information about how certain types of content are achieving their goals. This can allow them to adjust the balance of content and its presentation to better suit the taste of their readers. When editors see more directly what content their readers value, the worry is that news content will be commercialized – newsrooms only giving people what they want and neglecting what they also need.

In the Scandinavian context, these fears seem, however, to be somewhat exaggerated. When Karlsson and Clerwall (2013) looked into click metrics in Swedish newsrooms, they found that clicks have a limited effect on editorial priorities. The results of this early study also seem to hold. Editors are more concerned with providing a good mix of content rather than blindly following audience tastes. Although audience data can help marketing and advertising departments build better products for advertisers, editorial departments are still cautious about using these metrics towards personalization. First and foremost, the infrastructures that paywalls provide enable a transition towards digital income, giving newsrooms the tools they need to retain advertising revenue. The more news organizations know about their audience, the more attractive they become as advertising channels. What effect this may have on journalism – whether or not it may shift news values, move the content mix towards entertainment or gamify journalists towards clickbait journalism – remains to be seen.

Personalization

This process of "datafying" the audience relies on the use of algorithms. Digital subscription is what enables this tracking – not just within the walls of the news product, but also outside the news site context. Algorithms can track user behavior. They follow readers around and map patterns of engagement – how long users stay on a page, what content they click on, where the cursor moves, how far down they scroll on a page and where they go next. This data can be used to enhance user engagement on the site. The worry here is that algorithms will skew news content towards stories that gain traction on social media, which have a propensity for lifestyle, curiosities and human interest stories that generate shares. Another worry that the introduction of algorithms in the newsroom poses is how and to what extent journalists and editors understand what algorithms do and how to use them.

Algorithms can aid editors in personalizing content, particularly on the front page. Personalization entails adjusting content to personal preferences. This means increased value for the user, but it may also reduce the breadth and scope of the common space where audiences engage with the news agenda. Although this does not mean that everyone gets a different selection of news stories when they visit a news site, online news differentiation does entail a segmentation of audiences into the particular. Little is known what effects this may have on journalism or public deliberation, but it clearly changes the function of news media for audiences. When news sites are geared towards user interests, they are likely to attach higher value to the experience. On the other hand, part of the value of journalism is that news enables people to talk to each other about current events. Hence, although users may be getting a more personal experience from their news provider, one of the main values of journalism – topics that allow people to engage with each other – could take a back seat. In the search for more engagement-generated income, journalism may dilute its democratic value foundation – the common agenda that elevates journalism to a public good.

All the major Scandinavian news corporations and newspapers are working to develop personalization technologies and strategies. But there are few signs of a fully personalized future to date. Whereas experiments and the development of personalization algorithms are taking place in many newsrooms, editors and journalists remain cautious about taking personalization too far. For most of these news providers, personalization is only attached to certain kinds of content. Front pages may reflect user preferences, but editors can still override algorithmic priorities, and no readers can avoid getting major breaking news stories. In most cases, readers can also opt out of this service. Hence, personalization does not mean full automation.

The structural problem with personalization of online news is that this is difficult to implement for smaller newspapers. Most low-frequency, local newspapers produce rather few news stories – too few to prevent forming highly skewed news agendas if personalized. Large newspapers that produce over 100 news stories per day have enough variation in their content to generate data for analysis of performance and to prevent topical bias.

Moreover, low story output also means that top stories would become old news relatively quickly, making local news sites look one-sided and outdated. The development of digital subscription, algorithmic curation and user data is thus yet another sign of the massive advantage that corporate resources will have for journalism in the near future. Unless local newspapers find alternative avenues for sustaining their readership and generating value in audience engagement in this algorithmic news environment, they will likely need to seek corporate ownership to link up with the digital infrastructures needed to generate future income.

Content marketing

The structures surrounding digital journalistic production not only change the ways news organizations relate to their two main sources of income, advertisers and audiences. Digital disruptions are also changing journalism itself. Signs of market proximities in journalistic content can be seen in emerging forms of content marketing, in experiments with robot journalism and in highly disruptive forms of so-called fake news.

An added effect of the downturn in advertising income has been that news organizations themselves – in an effort to increase their value to advertisers – have developed advertising services of their own, closer to the journalistic product. Content marketing is essentially a technique for marketing goods and services in the shape of journalistic content. This new form of advertising has been criticized for looking too much like journalism, for not being sufficiently labeled as paid content, and thus for diluting trust in "real" journalism. The problem with this form of content is that readers find it difficult to spot the difference between sponsored content and regular journalism (Iversen & Knudsen, 2017). Moreover, the majority of this content is created within (or at least adjacent to) the journalistic organizations themselves. Several news organizations in Scandinavia have established content marketing divisions of their own. These do not necessarily challenge the historical and institutional division between marketing and editorial departments, but they do challenge the separation between advertising and editorial content. This is not least because paid content is designed to look like editorial content. Moreover, most of this content is produced by journalists (perhaps better described as former journalists) who utilize the form of news to shape advertising messages into the form of news stories commissioned by different kinds of companies (Barland, Bang, Krokan, & Viken, 2017; see also Lynch, 2018).

The value of content marketing – for advertisers and audiences as well as news organizations – is the form of news, or storytelling (Pulizzi, 2012). When advertising messages assume journalistic form, they capitalize on the signals that tell people they are looking at a news story – the genre traits that makes news look like news. Rather than slogans and models designed to sell a product by positive associations, content marketing entails creating content around certain products – lifestyle, hobby and recreation stories designed to create a purchasing mood for a class of products, such as groceries or fitness equipment. Branding content within a journalistic setting thus gains value from being associated with a particular news brand (e.g. Matteo & Dal Zotto, 2015). Not only are news organizations moving closer to the market by selling advertising space to these content marketing efforts, but they are actively involving their journalists in the production of non-journalistic content that looks like journalism. As such, the monetary value of branded content products lies not only with advertising revenue but also in jobs. If the boundary-protecting needs of the profession are to maintain a strong, visible division between real journalism and less real journalism, professionals who create content marketing are actively engaged in blurring these lines.

In Norway, the strongest defender of this new marketing activity has been VG, an early adapter in branded content that in 2015 established the subsidiary VG Partnerstudio, offering content marketing services. Scandinavian media companies have already gained a foothold in this new market – Bonnier's Spoon, Egmont's Sempro and Schibsted's Brand Studio all offer content marketing services. Moreover, these companies are hiring. VG has defended its need to branch out into this new service sector because it adds revenue to its operations. In experimenting with these new formats, the newspaper suffered both criticism and even a conviction of breach of the codes of ethics in the Norwegian press ethics council. Although news organizations' venture into content marketing has created conflict within these organizations and indeed within the profession – with critics arguing that attachment to content marketing hurts journalism's credibility – branded content is also proving to be a good source of revenue. The balancing act that news organizations have to perform here is one of demonstrating market distance. This is a difficult task, given that journalistic credibility – or the news brand – is essentially what is on sale in this market. Although journalism needs this added revenue to maintain good news operations, audiences may not necessarily see the difference or remain sympathetic to the financial needs of the organization. As long as people keep seeking news for free, and as long as they keep their ad blockers up to avoid annoying banner messages and other advertisements, news organizations need to seek revenue elsewhere – in this case, by cannibalizing their own credibility.

Content marketing has, however, well and truly established itself as part of the content readers encounter on news websites. Much of the controversy around it has also died down. To what extent it ultimately serves to hurt journalism's credibility remains to be seen. But it is yet another sign of the extent to which journalism is drawn towards the market in efforts to correct revenue imbalances in the digital advertising realm. On the other hand, the launch of "brand studios" is a sign that news organizations and publishers are innovating by embracing the fact that newspapers and publishers have brand value of their own that social media cannot match. If audience engagement is the way forward in value creation in online publishing and marketing, news sites are prime locations to attain this engagement. Moreover, advertisers are waking up to the fact that journalistic storytelling is a good way to generate loyalty, engagement and brand attachment. If nothing else, this more direct shift back to the journalistic packaging of commercial messages, which has sustained news media as a valuable advertising channel for centuries, has made up for the loss of the "eyeballs" value that traditional media used to hold for retailers wishing to reach potential customers.

Fake news

Another phenomenon that threatens to hurt journalism's credibility is fake news – misinformation intended to incite traffic and engagement online, either for political or financial gain (Bakir & McStay, 2018). Fake news is not a big problem in Scandinavia; at least, not on the scale seen in other countries, such as during the 2016 U.S. presidential election and the Brexit vote in the U.K. or during political processes in Eastern Europe and Southeast Asia. But there have been instances of what has been termed "junk" news, particularly in conjunction with the Swedish general election in 2018. Most junk news in a Scandinavian context concerns the topics of immigration, cultural relativism and Islam. Many of these stories are propagated by right-of-the-right online news sites and spread through social media. Sites such as *Samhällsnytt.se*, *Nyheteridag.se* and *Friatider.se* in Sweden and *Rights.no*, *FMI.no* and *SIAN.no* in Norway (see Figenschou & Ihlebæk, 2018) assume a newslike look and follow journalistic conventions making items appear to be news. The sites even assume newslike names such as "community news" and "news today". Many stories on these sites often use made-up statistics to make outrageous claims, for example, about when the country will have a majority immigrant (mainly Muslim) population, or to feed conspiracy theories about the hidden agendas of the established political elites.

The worry attached to the fake news phenomenon is, in Scandinavia as elsewhere, the concern that misinformation may lead to lower levels of trust in institutions, journalism being one of them. There is therefore mounting pressure on journalism to mark the difference between real and fake news. Scandinavian news organizations were quick to launch such boundary-demarcating efforts in the wake of the fake news phenomenon in the U.S. in the fall of 2016. Many of these fact-checking services are operated by established news organizations (see Graves & Cherubini, 2016). In Norway, *Faktisk.no* is an industry-wide collaboration funded by established news organizations in a joint effort to check statements made in the mainstream and fringe press alike. Fact checking, as such, serves a two-sided purpose. On the one hand, it performs a public service, alerting the public as to the veracity of the various statements, facts and statistics that form the foundation of public debate. On the other hand, it performs a legitimating function – for journalism as an expert profession with monopoly knowledge as well as for the publicist institution as the primary arbiter of facts.

Fake news is essentially a gaming strategy to elicit income from programmatic advertising. The online economy is based on clicks to generate revenue. Clicks generated from social media are driven by emotion – the things that make you angry and the things that make you laugh (Berger & Milkman, 2012). To generate traffic from social media, stories need to reach a high number of shares; hence, outrageous stories perform better – typically crime stories and curiosities, but also political stories and conspiracy theories. Before Google's advertising company AdSense was forced to adjust its algorithms to ensure that established brands like Volkswagen or McDonald's did not end up advertising on fake news sites – or worse, sites that actively incite hatred and mistrust – this click-based economy ensured that fake news could yield considerable revenue. Hence, the money-making strategies of the "fakers" that came to prominence in the winter of 2016–2017 were able to capitalize on journalism's genre traits to spread misinformation in the name of profit. Once the fault in the programmatic strategies of Google's advertising services and Facebook's trending topics was exposed, many of the problems of these financially motivated fake news sites went away. Left, however, is a playbook for attracting the attention of social media audiences to extremist political agendas, using journalism-like formats to package content.

The Swedish 2018 parliamentary elections served as a warning about the effects of misinformation in political campaigns. An Oxford Internet Institute report from 2018 (Hedman et al., 2018) showed that the amount of junk news during the Swedish election was higher than anywhere in Europe, and second only to the United States. Of news items shared on social media, the ratio of legacy media news stories to junk news stories were roughly two to one. The report found that misinformation had become a mainstream phenomenon in Sweden and, moreover, that most of this misinformation was home-grown (rather than Russian or otherwise foreign). The majority of the stories were generated by three fringe sites, *Samhällsnytt*, *Nyheter i dag* and *Fria tider*, largely focusing on immigration and Islam. The Swedish parliamentary election ended in a significant result for the immigration-hostile party the Swedish Democrats, leading to a hung process in which no coalition could be formed, essentially leaving Sweden without a government for several months. Although the link between junk news and the election results is by no means clear or necessarily probable, connections between party affiliates and these junk news sites have been established. To that end, the rise of populist political parties, with their animosity towards established media, and the rise of alternative, immigration-hostile news sites savvy in the use of social media are causing increasing concern across the Scandinavian political landscape.

The digital economy

Although the external forces causing a rise in fake news are largely politically motivated in the Scandinavian setting, the mechanisms that enable misinformation to go viral and thus shape public perceptions are shaped by the economy of the online news ecology. Hyperlinks form the backbone of this system. Visits to these sites generate advertising income. When users share links with each other, site visits increase, generating more income. Social media therefore has become an essential conduit to economic performance in the online realm. This is why news organizations have been so willing to share their content on social media – to generate traffic to their own sites. In a way, they have to. Journalism needs to be where the people are – and, hence, where the money is. But social media does not always function according to democratic ideals. People do not necessarily engage with content as citizens, ready to deliberate in an open, fact-based discourse. What Quandt (2018) terms “dark participation” – the flip side of the optimism that characterized early approaches to the potential democratic effects of audience participation resulting from opening journalism up to the world – signifies a sinister exploitation of journalism’s virtues (or, rather, its trusted brand power) for malicious, often populist or propagandistic, gains. But Quandt is careful to also caution the generalizability of the extent to which propaganda, hate speech and cyberbullying are taking over online journalism. Indeed, he warns against an either/or approach to the effects of participation. This welcomed balanced approach should also be extended to media’s economic interests. The diagnosis that journalism’s business interests – the potential to save money by inviting user-generated content and citizen participation in journalistic production – has contributed to these “dark” effects is indeed a dark view of media managers’ strategies. Again, money emerges as a force of evil.

It is important to remember, in this context, that revenue strategies in the news industries are not always so deliberate, nor are the effects necessarily so predictable. Money is, nevertheless, a necessity for fulfilling journalistic ideals. A Darwinian view would here see adaptation as the key to survival. Whoever can best adapt to their environment, and shape their existence according to the sources of sustenance available, wins. A biological view would thus expect the search for sustainability to shape behavior, culture and condition. If the resources that can sustain journalism in this context are indeed dark, then journalism itself becomes corrupted – a sick, twisted version of itself. But perhaps it is not the behavior of the starving journalist that should be under scrutiny, but rather the sustenance that journalism seeks – advertising revenue. Journalism studies have seen a turn towards the audience in recent years. No wonder – this is after all the big question for news organizations: where have our readers gone, and how do we get them back? This interest is in turn revenue-inspired. Audiences have stopped paying for news, and the effects are felt across the media industries. But rather than addressing the revenue question head-on, research has fixated solely on users and their behavior. "Saving" journalism has thus become a one-sided question, focusing on only one side of the two-sided business model. What has been neglected in this investigation is the advertising side of the equation. This is, after all, the true symbiosis in journalism's business model – an exchange of money for attention that benefits all three parties: news organizations, retailers and audiences alike.

The fact is that online advertising is rather stupid. Moreover, it has remained in a juvenile state for far too long. People hate the banner ads, static bars, video interruptions and repetitive YouTube ads that pollute their media content. Online advertising is something to be avoided. This is why about one quarter of users in Scandinavia use an ad blocker on their computers' browsers (Fletcher & Nielsen, 2017), a rate among the highest in the world. Rather than meeting advertising halfway, creating good environments and solutions for ads to add value to their product, online news media have failed to innovate their advertising spaces. Content marketing is filling some of this need, but advertisers have largely moved on, mainly to influencers – using social media as platforms to reach users rather than publicist environments. Hence, advertising has become more convoluted, hidden, less noticeable and more indirect than before. Not only has audience participation become "dark", but advertising is also growing murkier by the minute.

Journalism's primary market is audiences and advertisers. These targets have moved closer and more distant at the same time. To close a widening gap between themselves and their markets, news organizations are making efforts to internalize them. There used to be clear demarcations between news organizations and audiences. Now, news providers have invited users into their stories, into their comment sections and into their data repositories. Not only are newsrooms instantly informed on the performance of news stories; journalistic content is also increasingly personalized according to individual tastes. Moreover, news distribution has been left to the audience as news sharing on social media. The boundary between advertising and journalism also used to be visibly firm – marked clearly on the page or within and between programs. Now, commercial messages appear alongside the news, looking like journalism, inside the newsbar rather than outside as banner ads. News organizations do their own market research, form partnerships with brands and automate targeted marketing campaigns. The market pull on journalism is thus becoming more visible, not least in the journalistic product itself.

6 Conclusions

If journalism's problem is that it is positioned between political and economic forces from which it needs to keep its distance to retain institutional legitimacy, then which of these forces is worse? What kind of distance is required, and how close is too close? For that matter, if journalism is really approaching both fields at once, what does this mean for the institutional "middle"? Indeed, what constitutes this "middle"?

The previous chapters have discussed how journalism, in the context of digital disruption, finds itself increasingly attracted to the state and the market. Both of these attractions are essentially economic in nature. Journalism is searching for the resources to sustain itself. This is institutional behavior. Institutions' main aim is to sustain themselves as relevant, powerful and enduring. The institutional logic mobilized to attain such sustainability should be used to maintain jurisdictional boundaries. Journalism, however, encounters shifting rules and resources available to maintain institutional integrity. Within a profession, the right actions will always be those that serve to sustain its position. Journalism's professional ideology serves a particular purpose in this regard, given journalism's weak professional status – not requiring proper licensing like "true" professions. This is where the institutional middle lies – with journalistic ideology – basically the elements that support the argument that journalism is important for democracy and society. Whenever the profession is threatened by some external accusation (e.g. claims of political bias or commercialism) or internally by unethical behavior (the worst of which is falsifying stories), the typical traits of the profession – objectivity, facts, sources, editorial hierarchy, the wall between journalism and advertising – are mobilized to communicate what separates journalism from other types of activities. This is boundary maintenance (Carlson & Lewis, 2015) – demonstrations of professional integrity based on the norms and myths of the institution.

Although journalism has faced increasing external pressures threatening to disrupt its institutional boundaries – claims of leftism, fake news, bloggers, hackers, social media – these external forces are not quite as serious as internal disruptive behavior. External threats can always be encountered with boundary maintenance. This is why economic motives are often met with suspicion. Economic motives are internal motives – news organizations' search for self-sustainability beyond the professional. The dangers of economic motives have been one of the main foci of critical political economy research on journalism. Most of this research has, however, been conducted during journalism's most profitable era – in the 1980s and 1990s, when advertising revenues were soaring. The propensity of already-wealthy media owners to continually seek higher revenues contributed to the ownership concentration, commercialization and corporatization seen as damaging to journalism in this period. Hence, owners' and managers' visible search for higher profits is already framed as bad, based on prior experience, not least because it has threatened to undermine journalism's primary assets and especially if profit-seeing strategies lead to tabloidization, bias and commercialization. As a result, any time the profit motive becomes too visible, it hurts journalism. To that end, market proximity is worse than proximity to the state because market attractions are acted upon positively within news organizations, whereas state attractions rather have constituted external forces that produce boundary-protecting behavior. It is worse when journalism hurts itself because institutional ideology demands self-protection.

Journalism finds itself in a disruptive state because, as Ryfe (2017) remarks, there is less for the profession to push against. Not only is there less of a market to push against, journalism is exerting less pressure in the direction of the state. In fact, Scandinavian journalism is actively seeking more state intervention – whether by advocating for increased government support or seeking the active curtailment of public service broadcasting. Journalism needs private funding to sustain proper distance from the state. When this funding dissipates, it needs to seek other sources of revenue. As this revenue-seeking behavior becomes more visible, it presents more of a danger to institutional boundaries. Here it is important to note, however, that sustaining the financial viability of news organizations also constitutes institutional behavior. What are news owners and managers doing in this search, if not trying to sustain themselves? The fact is that this economic behavior has always been part of what marks journalism's boundaries – it is just that the revenues that news organizations seek today lie closer to the institutional walls than before, bringing journalism closer to the state and the market.

The question facing journalism within this disruption is how close is too close. This is a difficult question to answer. Already, content marketing may be a step too close. In some media systems, government support is entirely too close. In establishing the extent to which the walls of the profession are becoming too crowded in either direction – towards the state or towards the market – a mapping of the activities outside these boundaries is necessary. In assessing whether its actors are external or internal and analyzing the extent to which these activities compromise the assets that journalism has to defend itself against field destabilization – its institutional middle – the extent of journalism's problem can be gauged. This has been the aim of this analysis, to discover the distances left in journalism's state/market relationship within a media systems context. Media systems theory is important in this endeavor because the rules and resources at journalism's disposal are different in different national and regional contexts. And the rules and resources available to the profession depend upon the particularities of the system – its political system, the history of the press, its infrastructures and ownership patterns, editorial cultures and the role of the state in society.

In Scandinavia, the role of the state is largely seen as benevolent. This is a cornerstone of welfare state economics – cooperation between private, organizational and state interests. Within such a welfare state context, commerce, industry and private money can be a force for good – as long as private interests are in on the welfare state project. The welfare state idea is essentially one of positive externalities – one that says everyone is better off if everyone is included in, and contributes to, the system. Taxes are an essential part of this contract. Individuals and businesses pay taxes that the state uses to pay for the education and care of its citizens to ensure their productivity as workers, generating income for their employers, private business owners. Hence, when Google and Facebook evade taxes within this system, a certain socio-cultural gut reaction is produced. The media are part of this system of positive externalities. Taxes pay to sustain a diverse media landscape for the benefit of citizens' information, culture and deliberative needs, which ultimately strengthens democracy. Google and Facebook's tax evasion not only feels deeply unfair, it also upsets the contract: in exchange for stable financial welfare, you pay into the system.

To that end, Scandinavian media systems are moving towards protectionism. It is, after all, better to concentrate media and ownership power within the welfare state system than to leave it vulnerable to outside, neoliberalist vultures with pure profit motives. Hence, while Scandinavian media regulations have always been a mix of trade policy and cultural policy, the trade policy part of the framework is gaining in visibility and importance. This is not only because the largest media organizations are proposing a grim crisis narrative, shifting policy more towards the needs of business than of citizens; it is also because local newspapers – an essential part of the system – are in real danger of dying out unless they can latch on to the new, digital media economy. Media policy thus becomes a question of sustainability – how to secure the mixed model of private and state-supported media within the media welfare state.

In this context, journalism's movements towards the state and the market are connected. Because the state has always played a part in Nordic media welfare state systems, the connections between journalism and the state can also be mobilized when the market fails. Within this framework, Scandinavian media may be more robust in handling this increased closeness than in other parts of the world, essentially because state/market relationships have always been present here. Strong professional cultures coupled with the established arm's-length principle for state involvement have created certain expectations as to what acceptable distance means. This is why media systems theory is useful as a basis for this framework. Though all monies come with expectations, the state is legally bound to expect only that the journalism it supports is conducive to citizens' welfare. To that end, closeness to the state by way of financial support is not seen as quite as precarious in democratic corporatist systems as it may be in liberal systems, where state involvement is looked upon with more suspicion. Private money, in this context, is part of a different contract, one in which democratic welfare is not an obligation. As such, media systems theory helps unlock the basis of how institutions inter-operate, allowing for an analysis of proximities between journalism and other fields based on the rules and resources within the socio-political system in question.

Given this model, one should be able to establish the degree of disruption in various media systems to enable a diagnosis of the relative distance between journalism and the state/market system, to which an evaluation of the sustainability of these distances can be made. For journalism within the Scandinavian media systems, the following can be concluded from this analysis:

- Scandinavian journalism is moving closer to the state, seen in particular in its active seeking of increased state support for private media, its arguments for increased protectionism and its coordinated call for state curtailment of public service broadcasting.
- Scandinavian news media are also cautiously approaching the political field, seen in the rise of partisan, populist online media sites engaged in anti-immigration rhetoric.
- At the same time, journalism is moving closer to the market, not only through content marketing but also in its appropriation of user data to capitalize on programmatic advertising, personalization and online traffic generation.

To what extent do these state/market proximities present a problem for journalism? One major problem with journalism's proximity to the state lies with its attack on public service broadcasting. Curtailment of public service media – built and sustained for the benefit of citizens rather than the private market – endangers the mixed media model where the crowding-in effect (Nielsen et al., 2016) is particularly advantageous for private operators. Public service broadcasting has an educational effect (Aalberg, Van Aelst, & Curran, 2010). Because it entices people towards media consumption, it also benefits the earnings of private media. Public service media conditions people towards consumption of nationally produced current affairs reporting and entertainment, strengthening people's attachment to local media culture. Private media, in their efforts to make public service media the giant that stifles their profit potential, are only digging their own graves by pulling the rug out from under the national media landscape. Private media's problem is not strong public service broadcasting. Private media's problem is other private media: especially foreign, privately owned, global social media platforms. These are the media "stealing" their audiences and advertisers, not public service broadcasting.

The main problem with this market is that it will likely kill off local newspapers. The large, incumbent players that have the resources to innovate will survive this shift to the digital economy. With the emergence of audience metrics and programmatic advertising, the landscape for future earnings has become clearer, to the point where there is now a visible, probable source of sustainable revenue that capitalizes on the strengths of a journalistic environment, rather than some by-product of journalism. Small, independently owned media lack the resources to make this shift. The barriers to survival have grown higher, and they lie with the digital infrastructures that can ensure the partnerships necessary to capitalize on journalism's main asset in the digital era: its audiences.

If any remedies are to be suggested in this situation, they are the following:

- Governments should protect public service media. These are the cornerstones of profitable media markets where private operations can be sustained. They are also intended for the benefit of citizens rather than business. Dismantling what is essentially the ownership of the people is not a sound strategy to attach audiences to journalistic media.
- Governments should allow stronger concentration of ownership. Essentially, they should allow local independents to merge with larger corporations. In the event that local ventures fail to attract corporate buyers, governments should provide funding to subsidize local newspapers' shift to the algorithmic reality, sustaining the decentralized newspaper structures that are so central to the Scandinavian media and political

> systems. Ownership concentrations should be unproblematic for two reasons: first, they strengthen Scandinavian markets against foreign takeovers, and second, they pose no threat to media diversity. Newspaper holdings are so diverse within Scandinavian newspaper chains that corporate identity has little effect on content diversity (see Sjøvaag & Pedersen, 2018b). Moreover, the decentralized, monopolistic structure of newspaper markets ensures the heterogeneity needed to guarantee external media diversity. Because audiences are news organizations' main asset, local affiliation and a local journalistic social contract serve as diversifying forces on corporatization.

The main advantage of Scandinavian journalism is its welfare-based media system. Sustaining the characteristics of this system, to the extent that governments have the leverage to do so, is in the best interest of its citizens, to which media policy is directed. As with all welfare state economy, this partnership is beneficial for private media companies. Although journalism's problem – standing between the state and the market – is causing disruption in the news industries, this problem may also be a source of strength. As journalism loses legitimacy in the market, attracting less revenue from audiences and advertisers, private media has gained legitimacy in the state sector.

Strengths and weaknesses

The model proposed in this book can be used to analyze the state of journalism as an institution, detect shifts and movements and identify threats and risks. The strength of this framework is its flexibility, being nested in media system realities that face changes and disruptions that take hold within established system properties. Hallin and Mancini's (2004) media systems model bases such analyses in the state/media relationship. What has been attempted here is to introduce the market into this system on a more comprehensive scale, not just as a source of corruption but also as a natural and necessary foundation for journalism's legitimacy. As such, it offers an entry point to a more detached analysis of what markets do to journalism, using market realities to understand and describe changes and challenges to the journalistic profession. The weaknesses in this model, on the other hand, are threefold.

First, this model ignores the citizen, civil society and the audiences that journalism addresses. This has been deliberate mainly because journalism has little in the form of leverage here. Journalists cannot sanction audiences who reject their content. Audiences constitute a market, and market rules do not have the same reciprocity as the social contract. If people do not want to buy your product, they do not have to. Buyers do not have obligations to sellers in the same way voters have obligations to the state. To that end, people are here included in the sphere of the market, not as a separate sphere on their own.

Second, this analysis has wholeheartedly bought into the crisis narrative. In fact, it forms the basis of the entire investigation. The problem with this is not only that the crisis narrative is largely propagated by the industry itself – and in particular, private actors struggling to retain earnings – but also that the crisis narrative is predominantly an Anglo-American construct, a description of a reality that much better describes the state of liberal media systems than it does democratic corporatist systems. To that end, even though it assumes a Scandinavian welfare state perspective, this book participates in a generalization of journalism's current state rather than necessarily nuanced perspectives on journalism's crisis.

Third, this model is founded in the liberal, linear historical understanding of journalism. In this narrative, things tend to go from good to bad, markets tend to be emancipatory and states tend to be restrictive. Journalists tend to be heroes, and owners and editors are champions of democracy standing firmly on the side of citizens against tyranny and oppression. The problem with this understanding is that structures are often given less power than individual actors. Another problem is that solutions to problems are often found within a "more market, less state" equation.

This analysis has tried to mitigate these weaknesses by internalizing them. Audiences are included in the sphere of the market because this is journalism's primary asset and the main resource it is trying to retain. The crisis narrative is left unchallenged because this is the narrative that drives industry strategies and thus journalism's negotiation in the state/market relationship. And the liberal theoretical understanding is assumed because it forms the basis of journalism's self-understanding and thus the basis for how it encounters boundary challenges and protects itself as an institution, whether threats are internal or external.

In doing so, I hope I have added some small contribution to the theoretical framework for digital journalism studies. I am not suggesting this is the only way to see journalism – as a problematic position between the state and the market. But I do believe that the "problem" assumption is a fruitful one – and that states and markets remain binaries in which to analyze this problem – in analyzing what news media do to sustain the institution within an industry context where journalism has to make money in order to fulfill the social contract: and where private ownership remains a foundation of that contract.

References

Aalberg, T., Van Aelst, P., & Curran, J. (2010). Media systems and the political information environment: A cross-national comparison. *The International Journal of Press/Politics, 15*(3), 255–271.

Alexander, J. C. (2016). Introduction: Journalism, democratic culture, and creative reconstruction. In J. C. Alexander, E. B. Breese, & M. Luengo (Eds.), *The crisis of journalism reconsidered* (pp. 1–28). Cambridge: Cambridge University Press.

Allern, S. (1996). *Kildenes makt: Ytringsfrihetens politiske økonomi.* [*The power of source: The political economy of freedom of expression.*] Oslo: Pax.

Allern, S. (2011). PR, politics and democracy. *Central European Journal of Communication, 41*(6), 125–139.

Allern, S., & Ørsten, M. B. (2011). The news media as a political institution: A Scandinavian perspective. *Journalism Studies, 12*(1), 92–105.

Allern, S., & Pollack, E. (2017). Journalism as a public good: A Scandinavian perspective. *Journalism*. doi:10.1177/1464884917730945

Altschull, J. H. (1984). *Agents of power: The role of the news media in human affairs*. Harlow: Longman Publishing Group.

Altschull, H. J. (1997). Boundaries of journalistic autonomy. In D. Berkowitz (Ed.), *Social meanings of news* (259–268). Thousand Oaks: Sage.

Bagdikian, H. H. (2004). *The new media monopoly*. Boston, MA: Beacon Press.

Bakir, V., & McStay, A. (2018). Fake news and the economy of emotions: Problems, causes, solutions. *Digital Journalism, 6*(2), 154–175.

Baldasty, G. J. (1992). *The commercialization of news in the nineteenth century*. Madison: University of Wisconsin Press.

Barland, J. (2013). Innovation of new revenue streams in digital media. *Nordicom Review*, Special issue, 99–112.

Barland, J., Bang, T., Krokan, A., & Viken, M. (2017). *Innholdsmarkedsføring: Konsept, forretningsmodeller, juss, etikk og praksis.* [*Content marketing: Concept, business models, law, ethics and practice.*] Oslo: Damm.

Bastiansen, H. G. (2014). Rethinking mass communications in Norway: The neglected power of the centre-left alliance in the early 20th century and its importance until the present. *Nordicom Review, 35*(2).

Beam, R. A. (2001). Does it pay to be a market-oriented daily newspaper? *Journalism & Mass Communication Quarterly*, *78*(3), 466–483.

Benson, R. (2016). Institutional forms of media ownership and their modes of power. In M. Eide, H. Sjøvaag, & L. O. Larsen (Eds.), *Journalism re-examined: Digital challenges and professional reorientations* (pp. 29–47). Bristol: Intellect.

Benson, R., Blach-Ørsten, M., Powers, M., Willig, I., & Zambrano, S. V. (2012). Media systems online and off: Comparing the form of news in the United States, Denmark, and France. *Journal of Communication*, *62*(1), 21–38.

Benson, R., Powers, M., & Neff, T. (2017). Public media autonomy and accountability: Best and worst policy practices in 12 leading democracies. *International Journal of Communication*, *11*, 22.

Berger, Jonah and Kathrine. L. Milkman, 2012. "What Makes Online Content Viral?" *Journal of Marketing Research*. *49*(2): 192–205.

Blom-Hansen, J. (2000). Still corporatism in Scandinavia? A survey of recent empirical findings. *Scandinavian Political Studies*, *23*(2), 157–181.

Bondebjerg, I. (2016). PSB 3.0: TV and the digital and global challenge. *Nordicom Review*, *37*(2016), 185–191.

Bourdieu, P. (1984). *Distinction*. Cambridge, MA: Harvard University Press.

Brüggemann, M., Engesser, S., Büchel, F., Humprecht, E., & Castro, L. (2014). Hallin and Mancini revisited: Four empirical types of western media systems. *Journal of Communication*, *64*(6), 1037–1065.

Carey, J. (1989). *Communication as Culture: Essays on Media and Society*. Boston: Unwin Hyman.

Carlson, M., & Lewis, S. C. (Eds.) (2015). *Boundaries of journalism: Professionalism, practices and participation*. New York: Routledge.

Chadwick, A. (2017). *The hybrid media system: Politics and power*. Oxford: Oxford University Press.

Christians, C. G., Glasser, T., McQuail, D., Nordenstreng, K., & White, R. A. (2009). *Normative theories of the media: Journalism in democratic societies*. Urbana: University of Illinois Press.

Chyi, H. (2013). *Trial and error: US newspapers' digital struggles toward inferiority*. Pamplona: University of Navarra.

Cook, T. E. (1998). *Governing with the news: The news media as a political institution*. Chicago: University of Chicago Press.

COM. (2016/0593). *Proposal for a directive of the European Parliament and of the Council on copyright in the digital single market*. Brussels: Publications office of the European Union.

Couldry, H., & Hepp, A. (2012). Comparing media cultures. In F. Esser & T. Hanitzsch (Eds.), *Handbook of comparative communication research* (pp. 249–261). New York: Routledge.

Curran, J. (2005). Mediations of democracy. In J. P. Curran & M. Gurevitch (Eds.), *Mass Media and Society* (4th ed., pp. 122–149). London: Arnold.

Curran, J. (2012). Narratives of media history revisited. In M. Bailey (Ed.), *Narrating media history* (pp. 1–21). London: Routledge.

Curran, J. (2011). *Media and democracy*. London: Routledge.

Dahlberg, L. (2007). Rethinking the fragmentation of the cyberpublic: From consensus to contestation. *New Media & Society*, *9*(5), 827–847.

Davies, W. (2013). When is a market not a market? 'Exemption', 'externality' and 'exception' in the case of European state aid rules. *Theory, Culture & Society*, *30*(2), 32–59.

Dawes, S. (2014). Broadcasting and the public sphere: Problematising citizens, consumers and neoliberalism. *Media, Culture & Society*, *36*(5), 702–719.

Directive. (1989/552/ECC). *Council Directive of 3 October 1989 on the coordination of certain provisions laid down by law, regulation and administrative action in member states concerning the pursuit of television broadcasting activities.*

Directive. (2010/13/EU). *Directive of the European parliament and of the council of 10 March 2010 on the coordination of certain provisions laid down by law, regulation or administrative action in member states concerning the provision of audiovisual media services (Audiovisual media services directive).*

EC. (2018). *Telecommunications overview: European Commission*. Retrieved from http://ec.europa.eu/competition/sectors/telecommunications/overview_en.html

Eide, M. (2004). *Hodet på blokken: Essays om journalistikk.* [*Head on the block: Essays on journalism*.] Oslo: Gyldendal.

Engan, B. (2016). Et informert valg? Offentlighet, patriotisme og pressens lokale samfunnsoppdrag [An informed choice? Publicness, patriotism and the local social contract of the press.] *Norsk medietidsskrift*, *23*(2), 1–19.

Engelstad, F., Larsen, H., & Rogstad, J. (2017). The public sphere in the Nordic model. In F. Engelstad, H. Larsen, J. Rogstad, & K. Steen-Johnsen (Eds.), *Institutional change in the public sphere: Views on the Nordic model* (pp. 46–70). Berlin: De Gruyter.

Entman, R. M. (2005). Media and democracy without party competition. In J. P. Curran & M. Gurevitch (Eds.), *Mass media and society* (4th ed., pp. 251–270). London: Arnold.

Esping-Andersen, G. (1990). *The three worlds of welfare capitalism*. Princeton: Princeton University Press.

Ferrucci, P. (2018). Money matters? Journalists' perception of the effects of a weak market orientation. *Convergence*, *24*(4), 424–438.

Figenschou, T. U., & Ihlebæk, K. A. (2018). Challenging journalistic authority: Media criticism in far-right alternative media. *Journalism Studies*, 1–17.

Fletcher, R., & Nielsen, R. K. (2017). Are news audiences increasingly fragmented? A cross-national comparative analysis of cross-platform news audience fragmentation and duplication. *Journal of Communication*, *67*(4), 476–498.

Flew, T., & Waisbord, S. (2015). The ongoing significance of national media systems in the context of media globalization. *Media, Culture & Society*, *37*(4), 620–636.

Foucault, M. (2010). *The birth of biopolitics: Lectures at the College de France 1978–1979*. New York: Palgrave.

Freedman, D. (2005). Promoting diversity and pluralism in contemporary communication policies in the United States and the United Kingdom. *International Journal on Media Management*, *7*(1–2), 16–23.

Furhoff, L. (1967). *Upplagesspiralen.* [*The circulation spiral.*] Stockholm: Svenska Bokförlaget/Norstedts.

Gans, H. J. (2003). *Democracy and the news*. Oxford: Oxford University Press.

Garnham, N. (1986). The media and the public sphere. In G. Murdock, P. Golding, & P. Schlesinger (Eds.), *Communicating politics* (pp. 37–54). Leicester: Leicester University Press.

Garnham, N. (2014). The political economy of communication revisited. In J. Wasko, G. Murdock, & H. Sousa (Eds.), *The handbook of political economy of communications* (pp. 41–61). Malden: John Wiley & Sons.

Gieryn, T. F. (1983). Boundary-work and the demarcation of science from non-science: Strains and interests in professional ideologies of scientists. *American Sociological Review*, 781–795.

Giddens, A. (1984). *The constitution of society: Outline of the theory of structuration*. Cambridge: Polity.

Graves, L., & Cherubini, F. (2016). *The rise of fact-checking sites in Europe*. Oxford: Reuters Institute.

Habermas, J. (1971). *Borgerlig offentlighet – dens fremvekst og forfall. Henimot en teori om det borgerlige samfunn.* [*The structural transformation of the public sphere: An inquiry into a category of bourgeois society.*] Oslo: Gyldendal.

Habermas, J. (1994). Three normative models of democracy. *Constellations*, *1*(1), 1–10.

Habermas, J. (2009). *Europe: The faltering project*. Cambridge: Polity.

Hall, P. A., & Soskice, D. (2001). *Varieties of capitalism: The institutional foundations of comparative advantage*. Oxford: Oxford University Press.

Hall, P. A., & Taylor, R. C. (1996). Political science and the three new institutionalisms. *Political Studies*, *44*(5), 936–957.

Hallin, D. C. (1994). *We keep America on top of the world: Television journalism and the public sphere*, New York: Routledge.

Hallin, D. C., & Mancini, P. (2004). *Comparing media systems: Three models of media and politics*. Cambridge: Cambridge University Press.

Hallin, D. C., & Mancini, P. (2012). Conclusion. In D. C. Hallin & P. Mancini (Eds.), *Comparing media systems beyond the Western world* (pp. 278–304). Cambridge: Cambridge University Press.

Hallin, D. C., & Mancini, P. (2017). Ten years after comparing media systems: What have we learned? *Political Communication*, *34*(2), 155–171.

Hardy, J. (2008). *Western media systems*. London: Routledge.

Hardy, J. (2012). Comparing media systems. In F. Esser & T. Hanitsczh (Eds.), *The handbook of comparative communication research* (pp. 185–206). London: Routledge.

Harrie, E. (2018). *Newspapers in the Nordic media landscape*. Gothenburg: Nordicom.

Hedman, F., Sivnert, F., Kollanyi, B., Narayanan, V., Neudert, L., & Howard, P. N. (2018). *News and political information consumption in Sweden: Mapping the 2018 Swedish general election on Twitter. Data Memo 2018.3*. Oxford: Project on Computational Propaganda. Retrieved from http://comprop.oii.ox.ac.uk/research/sweden-election/

Held, D. (2002). Law of states, law of peoples: Three models of sovereignty. *Legal Theory*, *8*(2), 1–44.

Hjarvard, S. (2007). Den politiske presse: En analyse af danske avisers politiske orientering. [The political press: An analysis of Danish newspapers' political orientation.] *Journalistica: Tidsskrift for forskning i journalistik*, *2*(5), 27–53.

Hjarvard, S., & Kammer, A. (2015). Online news: Between private enterprise and public subsidy. *Media, Culture & Society*, *37*(1), 115–123.

Holand, A. M. (2013). Et delt mediemarked: Prosesser som fremmer små aviser. *Journalistica: Tidsskrift for Forskning i journalistik*, *1*, 52–73.

Holmes, S. (1990). Liberal constraints on private power? Reflections on the origins and rationale of access regulation. In J. Lichtenberg & D. MacLean (Eds.), *Democracy and the mass media: A collection of essays* (pp. 21–65). Cambridge: Cambridge University Press.

Høst, S. (2018). *Avisåret 2017*. Report no. 86/2018. Volda: Høgskulen i Volda.

Hovden, J. F. (2012). A journalistic cosmology: A sketch of some social and mental structures of the Norwegian journalistic field. *Nordicom Review*, *33*(2), 57–76.

Humphreys, P. (2012). A political scientist's contribution to the comparative study of media systems in Europe: A response to Hallin and Mancini. In N. Just & M. Puppis (Eds.), *Trends in communications policy research* (pp. 157–176). Bristol: Intellect.

IAB. (2018). *Digital brand advertising and measurement: IAB Europe*. Report June. Retrieved from www.iabeurope.eu/wp-content/uploads/2018/06/IAB-Europe-Digital-Brand-Advertising-and-Measurement-Report_June-2018.compressed.pdf

Ihlen, Ø., Skogerbø, E., & Allern, S. (2015). På jakt etter norsk politisk kommunikasjon-Kommentarartikkel. *Norsk Medietidsskrift*, *22*(03), 1–13.

Iversen, T. (2006). Capitalism and democracy. In B. R. Weingast & D. A. Wittman (Eds.) *The Oxford handbook of political science* (pp. 601–623). Oxford: Oxford University Press.

Iversen, M. H., & Knudsen, E. (2017). When politicians go native: The consequences of political native advertising for citizens' trust in news. *Journalism*. doi:10.1177/1464884916688289

Iversen, T., & Stephens, J. D. (2008). Partisan politics, the welfare state, and three worlds of human capital formation. *Comparative Political Studies*, *41*(4–5), 600–637.

Jacka, E. (2003). "Democracy as defeat": The impotence of arguments for public service broadcasting. *Television & New Media*, *4*(2), 177–191.

Kammer, A. (2016). A welfare perspective on Nordic media subsidies. *Journal of Media Business Studies*, *13*(3), 140–152.

Karlsson, M., & Clerwall, C. (2013). Negotiating professional news judgment and "clicks". *Nordicom Review*, *34*(2), 65–76.

Kiesow, D. (2018, February 19). *What it takes to shift a news organization to reader revenue*. American Press Institute. Retrieved from www.americanpressinstitute.org/reader-revenue/what-it-takes-to-shift-a-news-organization-to-reader-revenue/single-page/

Knudsen, E., Iversen, M. H., & Vatnøy, E. (2018). Mistillit til den andre siden. [Distrust towards the other side.] *Norsk Medietidsskrift*, *25*(02), 1–20.
Krumsvik, A. H. (2014). Mulige modeller for fordeling av nettinntekter. [Possible models for distribution of online revenue.] *Norsk Medietidsskrift*, *21*(02), 138–155.
Krumsvik, A. H. (2018). Redefining user involvement in digital news media. *Journalism Practice*, *12*(1), 19–31.
KUM. (2018). *Mediaftale for 2019–2023.* [*Media agreement for 2019–2023.*] Retrieved from www.regeringen.dk/media/5470/29062018endelig-medieaftale-2019-2023.pdf
Lacy, S. (1993). Understanding & serving readers: The problem of fuzzy market structure. *Newspaper Research Journal*, *14*(2), 55–67.
Lacy, S., & Sohn, A. B. (2011). Market journalism. In W. Lowrey & P. J. Gade (Eds.), *Changing the news: The forces shaping journalism in uncertain times* (pp. 159–176). London: Routledge.
Larsen, H. (2016). The crisis of public service broadcasting reconsidered: Commercialization and digitalization in Scandinavia. In J. C. Alexander, E. B. Breese, & M. Luengo (Eds.), *The crisis of journalism reconsidered* (pp. 43–58). Cambridge: Cambridge University Press.
Livingstone, S. (2012). Challenges to comparative research in a globalizing media landscape. In F. Esser & T. Hanitzsch (Eds.) *The handbook of comparative communication research* (pp. 415–429). New York: Routledge.
Lund, A. B. (2016). A stakeholder approach to media governance. In G. F. Lowe & C. Brown (Eds.) *Managing media firms and industries* (pp. 103–120). Heidelberg: Springer International Publishing.
Lund, A. B., & Berg, C. E. (2009). Denmark, Sweden and Norway: Television diversity by duopolistic competition and co-regulation. *International Communication Gazette*, *71*(1–2), 19–37.
Lund, A. B., & Lowe, G. F. (2013). Current challenges to public service broadcasting in the Nordic Countries. In U. Carlson (Ed.), *Public service media from a Nordic horizon: Politics, markets, programming and users* (pp. 51–73). Gothenburg: Nordicom.
Lunt, P., & Livingstone, S. (2012). *Media regulation: Governance and the interests of citizens and consumers*. Los Angeles: Sage.
Lynch, L. (2018). *Native advertising: Advertorial disruption in the 21st century news feed.* London: Routledge.
March, J. G., & Olsen, J. P. (1984). The new institutionalism: Organizational factors in political life. *The American Political Science Review*, *78*(3), 734–749.
Mathisen, B. R. (Ed.) (2010). *Lokaljournalistikk: Blind patriotisme eller kritisk korrektiv?* [*Local journalism: Blind patriotism or critical corrective?*] Kristiansand, Norway: Høyskoleforlaget.
Matteo, S., & Dal Zotto, C. (2015). Native advertising, or how to stretch editorial to sponsored content within a transmedia branding era. In *Handbook of media branding* (pp. 169–185). Springer, Cham.
McChesney, R. W. (2003). The problem of journalism: A political economic contribution to an explanation of the crisis in contemporary US journalism. *Journalism Studies*, *4*(3), 299–329.

McChesney, R. W. (2004). *The problem of the media: US communication politics in the twenty-first century*. New York: NYU Press.
McChesney, R. W. (2007). *Communication revolution: Critical junctures and the future of media*. New York: The New Press.
McManus, J. H. (1994). *Market-driven journalism: Let the citizen beware?* London: Sage.
McQuail, D. (1998). Commercialisation and beyond. In D. McQuail & K. Siune (Eds.), *Media policy: Convergence, concentration and commerce*. London: Sage.
McQuail, D. (2003). *Media accountability and freedom of publication*. Oxford: Oxford University Press.
Meehan, E. R., & Torre, P. J. (2014). Markets in theory and markets in television. In J. Wasko, G. Murdock, & H. Sousa (Eds.), *The handbook of political economy of communications* (pp. 62–82). Hoboken: John Wiley & Sons,
Meijer, I. C. (2001). The public quality of popular journalism: Developing a normative framework. *Journalism Studies*, *2*(2), 189–205.
Moe, H., & Mjøs, O. J. (2013). The arm's length principle in Nordic public broadcasting regulation. In U. Carlsson (Ed.), *Public service media from a Nordic horizon: Politics, markets, programming and users* (pp. 75–92). Gothenburg: Nordicom.
Mouffe, C. (2000). *The democratic paradox*. New York: Verso.
Mosco, V. (2009). *The political economy of communication* (2nd ed.). Los Angeles: Sage.
Murdock, G. (1993). Communications and the constitution of modernity. *Media, Culture & Society*, *15*(4), 521–539.
Nechushtai, E. (2018). From liberal to polarized liberal? Contemporary US news in Hallin and Mancini's typology of news systems. *The International Journal of Press/Politics*, *23*(2), 183–201.
Newman, N., Fletcher, R., Kalogeropoulos, A., Levy, D. A., & Nielsen, R. K. (2017). *Reuters institute digital news report*. Oxford: Reuters Institute.
Nielsen, R. K. (2016). The many crises of Western journalism: A comparative analysis of economic crises, professional crises, and crises of confidence. In J. C. Alexander, E. B. Breese, & M. Luengo (Eds.), *The crisis of journalism reconsidered* (pp. 77–97). Cambridge: Cambridge University Press.
Nielsen, R. K., Fletcher, R., Sehl, A., & Levy, D. (2016). *Analysis of the relation between and impact of public service media and private media*. Oxford: Reuters Institute.
Nilssen, C. S. (2013). Introduction: What's so special about Nordic public service media? In U. Carlson (Ed.), *Public service media from a Nordic horizon: Politics, markets, programming and users* (pp. 9–16). Gothenburg: Nordicom.
Nored. (2018). *Pressemelding fra norsk redaktørforening*. [*Press release from the Association of Norwegian Editors*.] Retrieved from www.nored.no/Redaktoernyheter/Pressemelding-fra-Norsk-Redaktoerforening
Norris, P. (2009). Comparative political communications: Common frameworks or Babelian confusion? *Government and Opposition*, *44*(3), 321–340.
North, D. (1990). Institutions and their consequences for economic performance. In K. S. Cook & M. Levi (Eds.), *The limits of rationality* (pp. 383–401). Chicago: The University of Chicago Press.

NOU. (1995:3). *Mangfold I media: Om eierskapskonsentrasjon i massemedia.* [*Media diversity: On ownership concentration in the mass media.*] Oslo: Ministry of Culture.

NOU. (2017:7). *Det norske mediemangfoldet: En styrket mediepolitikk for borgerne* [*Norwegian media diversity: A strengthened media policy for citizens.*] Oslo: The Ministry of Culture.

Nygren, G., Leckner, S., & Tenor, C. (2018). Hyperlocals and legacy media: Media ecologies in transition. *Nordicom Review*, *39*(1), 33–49.

Ohlsson, J. (2013). De svenska tidningsstiftelserna: Partipressens sista bastion? [The Swedish newspaper foundations: The last stand of the party press?] *Journalistica*, *1*, 10–32.

Ohlsson, J., & Facht, U. (2017). *Kampen om reklamen* [*Advertising wars.*] Gothenburg: Nordicom.

Ohlsson, J., & Sjøvaag, H. (2018). Protectionism vs. non-interventionism: Two approaches to media diversity in commercial terrestrial television regulation. *Javnost/The Public*, 1–19.

Örnebring, H. (2010). Technology and journalism-as-labour: Historical perspectives. *Journalism*, *11*(1), 57–74.

Ørsten, M. B., Willig, I., & Pedersen, L. H. (2017). PR, lobbyism and democracy: Mapping the revolving door in Denmark from 1981 to 2015. *NORDICOM Review: Nordic Research on Media and Communication*, *38*(2), 1G–1G.

Ostini, J., & Ostini, A. Y. (2002). Beyond the four theories of the press: A new model of national media systems. *Mass Communication and Society*, *5*(1), 41–56.

Ottosen, R., & Krumsvik, A. H. (2012). Digital challenges on the Norwegian media scene. *Nordicom Review*, *33*(2), 43–55.

Peterson, R. A., & Anand, N. (2004). The production of culture perspective. *Annual Review of Sociology*, *30*, 311–334.

Pfetsch, B., & Esser, F. (2012). Comparing political communication. In F. Esser & T. Hanitzsch (Eds.), *The handbook of comparative communication research* (pp. 25–47). New York: Routledge.

Picard, R. G. (1985). *The press and the decline of democracy: The democratic socialist response in public policy*. Westport, CT: Greenwood Publishing Group.

Pickard, V. (2017). Rediscovering the news: Journalism studies' three blind spots. In P. J. Boczkowski & C. W. Anderson (Eds.), *Remaking the news: Essays on the future of journalism scholarship in the digital age* (pp. 47–60). Cambridge, MA: MIT Press.

Powers, M., & Benson, R. (2014). Is the internet homogenizing or diversifying the news? External pluralism in the US, Danish, and French press. *The International Journal of Press/Politics*, *19*(2), 246–265.

Pulizzi, J. (2012). The rise of storytelling as the new marketing. *Publishing Research Quarterly*, *28*(2), 116–123.

PwC. (2017). *Unequal taxation in a digital world: A challenge for the Nordic media industry*. PwC. Retrieved from www.medialiitto.fi/files/4223/PwC_rapport_mediebedriftene.pdf

Quandt, T. (2018). Dark participation. *Media and Communication*, *6*(4), 36–48.

Raeijmaekers, D., & Maeseele, P. (2015). Media, pluralism and democracy: What's in a name? *Media, Culture & Society*, *37*(7), 1042–1059.

Regjeringen. (2017, April 25). *Uttalelse om utviklingen i et digitalisert mediemarked fra de nordiske kulturministre* [*Statement on the developments of a digitized media marked from the Nordic ministers of culture.*] Svalbard: Regjeringen.

Rokkan, S. (1967). Geography, religion, and social class: Crosscutting cleavages in Norwegian politics. In S. M. Lipset & S. Rokkan (Eds.), *Party systems and voter alignments: Cross-national perspectives* (pp. 379–386). New York: Free Press.

Ryfe, D. M. (2006). The nature of news rules. *Political Communication, 23*(2), 203–214.

Ryfe, D. M. (2017). *Journalism and the public*. Hoboken: John Wiley & Sons.

Schudson, M. (2008). *Why democracies need an unlovable press*. Cambridge: Polity.

Schudson, M. (2011). *The sociology of news* (2nd ed.). New York: W. W. Norton & Company.

Schultz, I. (2007). Fra partipresse over omnibuspresse til segmentpresse. *Journalistica-Tidsskrift for forskning i journalistik, 2*(5).

Scott, W. R. (1995). *Institutions and organizations*. Newbury Park: Sage.

Shoemaker, P. J., Vos, T. P., & Reese, S. D. (2009). Journalists as gatekeepers. In K. Wahl-Jorgensen & T. Hanitzsch (Eds.), *The handbook of journalism studies* (pp. 73–87). New York: Routledge.

Siebert, F. S., Peterson, T., & Schramm, W. (1956). *Four theories of the press: The authoritarian, libertarian, social responsibility, and Soviet communist concepts of what the press should be and do*. Urbana: University of Illinois Press.

Sjøvaag, H. (2015). The emergence of metropolitan news. *Nordicom Review, 36*(2), 17–32.

Sjøvaag, H., & Krumsvik, A. H. (2018). In search of journalism funding: Scenarios for future media policy in Norway. *Journalism Practice, 12*(9), 1201–1219.

Sjøvaag, H., Pedersen, T. A., & Owren, T. (2018). Is public service broadcasting a threat to commercial media? *Media, Culture & Society*, doi: 0163443718818354.

Sjøvaag, H., & Pedersen, T. A. (2018a). The effect of direct press support on the diversity of news content in Norway. *Journal of Media Business Studies*, 1–17.

Sjøvaag, H., & Pedersen, T. A. (2018b). Female voices in the news: Structural conditions of gender representations in Norwegian newspapers. *Journalism & Mass Communication Quarterly*. doi:10.1177/1077699018789885

Sjøvaag, H., Stavelin, E., Karlsson, M., & Kammer, A. (2018). The hyperlinked Scandinavian news ecology: The unequal terms forged by the structural properties of digitalisation. *Digital Journalism*. doi:10.1080/21670811.2018.1454335

Skogerbø, E. (1997). The press subsidy system in Norway: Controversial past – Unpredictable Future? *European Journal of Communication, 12*(1), 99–118.

Slaatta, T. (2015). Print versus digital in Norwegian newspapers. *Media, Culture & Society, 37*(1), 124–133.

SLKS. (2017). *Mediernes udvikling i Danmark: Globaliseringen af den danske mediebranch.* [*Media developments in Denmark: The globalisation of the Danish media industries.*] Copenhagen: Slots- og kulturstyrelsen.

Solvoll, M. (2017). *Annonse+ Annonsepotensialet for digitale lokalaivser med brukerbetaling.* [*Ads+ The advertising potential of digital local newspapers with user payment.*] Report no. 2. Oslo: BI.

SOU. (2015:94). Medieborgarna og medierna: En digital värld av rättigheter, skyldigheter, möjligheter och ansvar. [*Media citizens and the media: A digital world of rights, obligations, opportunities and responsibilities.*] Stockholm: Kulturdepartementet.

SOU. (2016:80). *En Gränsöverskridande mediepolitik: För upplysning, engagement och ansvar.* [*A transboundary media policy: For enlightenment, engagement and responsibility.*] Stockholm: Kulturdepartementet.

SOU. (2017:79). *Finansiering av public service: För ökad stabilitet, legitimitet och stärkt oberoende.* [*Financing public service: For increased stability, legitimacy and strong independence.*] Stockholm: Kulturdepartementet.

SOU. (2018:50). *Et oberoende public service för alla: Nya möjuligheter och ökat ansvar.* [*An independent public service for all: New possibilities and increased responsibilities.*] Stockholm: Kulturdepartementet.

Svensson, E. M., & Edström, M. (2016). Market-driven challenges to freedom of expression and the interaction between the state, the market, and the media. *Nordicom Review, 37*(2), 1–16.

Syvertsen, T., Mjøs, O. J., Moe, H., & Enli, G. S. (2014). *The media welfare state: Nordic media in the digital era.* Ann Arbor: University of Michigan Press.

Taylor, J. B. (2007). *Economics* (5th ed.). New York: Houghton Mifflin.

Thompson, J. B. (1995). *The media and modernity: A social theory of the media.* Cambridge: Polity.

Wadbring, I. (2007). The role of free dailies in a segregated society. *Nordicom Review, 28.*

White Paper 15 (2016–2017). *Et moderne og framtidsretta NRK – finansiering og innhaldsplikter.* [*A modern and forward-looking NRK: Financing and content provisions.*] Oslo: Kulturdepartementet.

Zelizer, B. (2004). *Taking journalism seriously: News and the academy.* Thousand Oaks: Sage.

Index

9781032338439